YES,
I BELONG
Here

YES, I BELONG Here

A Novel

DHIR DAYAL

ARCHWAY
PUBLISHING

Archway Publishing books may be ordered through booksellers or by contacting:

Archway Publishing
1663 Liberty Drive
Bloomington, IN 47403
www.archwaypublishing.com
844-669-3957

ISBN: 978-1-6657-3386-1 (sc)
ISBN: 978-1-6657-3385-4 (e)

Library of Congress Control Number: 2022921577

Print information available on the last page.

Archway Publishing rev. date: 12/20/2022

"What if you could go back
in time and make
a different set of mistakes?
Will you still be where you are?"
—My father, LSK

. . . . .

To
Angelic Americans
Everywhere!

. . . . .

I want to thank Aimee Reff, Valerie Cable, Tyler Hardin, and the entire team at Archway Publishing. Special thanks go to anonymous "Holly" who painstakingly combed through and unsnarled the narratives of selected chapters. Editorial department's Kira Axsiom provided indispensable assistance in clarifying last-minute issues arising out of certain evolving word usage and in the correct handling of block quotes. And thanks especially to Bob DeGroff for meritoriously completing the design phase. Next, Scott Crenshaw's efforts at finding a suitable way to market this product was commendable.

PROLOGUE

Most authors write either for the subject's sake as if it were a pastime, or for creating a literature because it earns them fame. Writing has proven to be cathartic for me. During what is sure to be the end of my long life, I have resorted to seeking diversion from either feeling wronged, or being given special fixes. It is a tactic not just of a victimizer in reverse, but as a mirror for those of ill will. Indeed, it conveys my imaginations, amusements, and inspirations, for future foreign students who might benefit from managing their life in an alien realm that they would find radically different from their own motherland. If one gains a valuable diversion, as this author has in composing this work, then that is a genuinely unique and salient discovery. All such imperative stories, imagined or probable, pertaining to the life of a student from abroad in North America, must be uncovered. In essence, this book is designed to be a cultural history of a dynamically evolving society.

Before Covid-19, when this manuscript was near completion, foreign students totaled about one million in the U.S. alone, comprising five percent of total enrollment in major universities. The majority of those were from China and India. Foreign students add about fifty billion dollars to the American economy that creates half a million jobs. Nonetheless, the traffic goes both ways: one in ten American youth goes abroad for studies.

More than ninety-six percent of students surveyed recently articulated that studying abroad increased their self-confidence. For me it opened my educational opportunities and career prospects.

Intangible impacts of studying abroad enabled me to gain an enhanced understanding of my own cultural values, personal biases, religious beliefs, and world view. Studying in a foreign country is an adventure though. It is not for the weak of heart.

Studying abroad, coupled with financial aid, is an incredible way to gain priceless real-world experience. We may find that only an international program can offer a tangible expertise we desire in our education.

For example, studying in North America can equip young people from former knowledge starved colonized countries to acquire advanced food production and marketing techniques based on scientific methods. Italy has awesome cuisine culture, romantic language, amazing art, and a dynamic history. It is the most sought-after destination for aspiring study abroad students. Study abroad programs in Italy offer a unique blend of Italian cultural studies and courses in variety of majors. Germany has immense opportunities for studying business, hard sciences, and it is a prodigious place for academic internships, with head offices of some of the world's biggest companies that are dedicated to innovation. Efficiency is high inside and outside of the classroom. One learns how to save time and reduce the bureaucratic inconveniences. The Hong Kong University of Science and Technology is a distinguished research institution of global renown. University of Kuala Lumpur is recognized professionally by various international bodies. It is the first infrastructure university in Malaysia that offers pathways to top universities in the United Kingdom and Australia. Many of its lecturers are industry-experts.

No matter where foreign students end up enrolling, they will be exposed to new cultures and experiences far beyond their expectations. It would take their communication, collaboration, and problem-solving skills to a much higher level. Hence, mind-expanding opportunities can be some of the greatest benefits of studying abroad.

Studying abroad affords us with the opportunity to intentionally mirror our skills and decide how we want to use them in a professional context anywhere in the world. Foreign education and experience often rank high among many employers—a critical asset for prospective employees. It shows that we are globally minded, appreciate diversity, and are resourceful and adventurous. It also shows that we would have the opportunity to interact and communicate with those with a different cultural background. Together, all of it means that our future job prospects will not only be promising, but also extensive in variety.

As a former foreign student, I plan to convey via these essays, my serendipitous encounters and describe my stint to future foreign students who might benefit in monitoring their own life in a country that offers a multiplicity of opportunities. America offers a great promise. These students are often stunned into moments of fortune as well as veiled cracks that were not expected but were remarkably valuable in charting their educational accomplishments. Truly it was to capture those ups and downs that formed the narrative for this book. Someone would surely write a comparable treatise on American foreign students who have studied abroad. At a minimum, the goal in this work is to guide and amuse future foreign students. At times, possibly it would create an aura of surrealism for them.

On our life's journey in a foreign country, we stumble upon situations that we least expect. We experience vivacity that was not predictable, or even expected. When we visit new places, we anticipate certain things that were sure to occur based on other people's narratives. But it seems that every visitor to a foreign land finds something far from the known. These can cause precarious detours. Amazing experiences can provide thrills if they are pleasant or non-threatening. Or these alien experiences can also expose them to a treacherous, expensive, and punishing detour.

Such dumb luck is certainly serendipitous. We do not possess super intelligence, at least at a younger age, to foresee when we might encounter new events that are either thrilling, startling, or horrid. Often, it just happens accidentally; but if we trust in the Divine Providence, our destiny will not be as calamitous as it could otherwise be.

During my journey to and long stay in North America, I encountered events, episodes, and people by chance the outcome of which I was not pursuing. The result of any resolve or quest can be serendipitous. Serendipity describes the happenstance, an accidentally acquired knowledge that might fortuitously bring good fortune.

America offered a great promise as told by former visitors and as was notably flashed in Hollywood movies. During a normal course of steering a student life in North American universities, a foreign student does what any young person would do—study the prescribed subject matter, learn about new customs, make friends, and stay away from the bigots who detest you. However, one is bound to encounter new situations and while doing so they are often stunned into moments of fortune. Notably, these are the experiences that were not expected but were remarkably valuable in charting the course of any one's educational accomplishments. Truly, it was to capture those likely ups and downs that constituted the theme for this book.

In composing this book, I have learned that positive discoveries were not only valuable in developing survival skills but helped me refine my beliefs that reinforced my capacity as a student to grow sets of antennas that led to clues for overcoming dreadful events. From there on, I became part of an unfolding story—the story was about me, and visitors like me. One can take it wherever one wants it to go. Also, I realized that something exists by itself independent of who we are, or the society we inhabit. The society is always evolving and since we are attached to it, we must go forward with it. Then we truly belong and have a place in it.

Certainly, an error of judgment could lead us to a different path, but even a mistake can be transformed into a desirable breakthrough because of a hidden force. It is akin to salvaging the past. Chance encounters do yield new insights based on openness and keen observation of one's eminence. Others could tell you how to live your life of conformity, but you have to choose a path to progress by yourself as it suits your temperament. Although human beings have a short life in which to experience diverse paths, collectively sundry experiences can be collated and a pattern found that would become a guidepost. One day we might stumble upon that knowledge and craft a tool that would enable us to avoid getting lost in spite of our best efforts. That would be a real boring path though. At times we should just get lost in order to discover what is new and desirable.

The author of *Fear of Flying* was asked if it bothered her when the readers assumed that her novel was simply an autobiography. Thereupon, Erica Jong replied that since that novel was written in 1973 the line between autobiography and fiction has blurred. Indeed, *Fear of Flying* was at the forefront of this trend. So was Geoff Dyer's *Jeff in Venice, Death in Varanasi*. There is an intense and flourishing field of popular American auto fiction that includes Ayad Akhtar's brilliantly crafted *Homeland Elegies*. In fact, Akhtar follows an established genre of postmodern American literature, also known as "realistic fiction."

It seems no one writes a literal biography anymore. That would indeed be a sterile reading. More often only fiction could be told because people would not believe certain truth. However, except for the surreal indulgences and irrational claims of glory, a serious memoirist follows a journey that is far from being mythical. Sometimes, though, life affords you incidents that even fiction writers cannot possibly imagine.

While novelists are free to invent their stories, they must discover a suitable path to communicate their narratives. This process can be weighed down because it requires sifting through a plethora of stories. The hope is to find those that are worth telling. One question begs an answer continuously: *Will it resonate with a wider meaning beyond the narrative's specific circumstance?* This question always lurks in the melancholy spaces of a fiction writer's mind. But a genuine story, no matter what, emerges that inevitably touches the hearts of earnest readers.

A narrative such as this purports to be a form of novel using auto-fiction technique, or the merging of autobiographical and possibly unforeseen milieus for the moment. This literary technique is distinguished from an autobiography by the proviso of bordering on a fiction. Names and locations have been suitably changed and events are recreated to make them more theatrical, yet the crux of the story may still bear a close resemblance to that of the author's life, or someone who becomes a part of his, or both. While the events of the life's twist of fate are recounted, there is no pretense of strict veracity. Presentation of events may be arranged only for artistic or thematic purposes. But the essential elements of the episode remain intact. Novels that portray situations with which the author is familiar are not necessarily autobiographical. Nor are novels that include aspects drawn from the author's life as minor plot details. To be considered an autobiographical novel by most standards, there must be a central character modeled after the author and an essential leitmotif that sequentially mirrors events in her or his life. Events described here are not necessarily out of the ordinary. Countless novels about private experiences such as family conflicts, serious debacles, and sex are written as autobiographical.

Suffice it to say, I left India for the West a decade after my country's independence from the lingering and torturous British rule. There indeed was a confluence between my joint family's autocratic rule, and the structure outside, that was also oppressive. Overbearing as both were, they differed in how they impacted the younger generation. For me, the former was more repelling than the latter. So, my choice was obvious. I decided to get away from the clutches of my own kinfolk when the opportunity arose.

After I boarded an airplane in Mumbai for London and settled in my seat after the take-off, I was overcome by a burst of emotion and tears started to streak down my cheeks. Suddenly, it dawned on me that I had embarked upon an enormous task riddled with risks and innumerable hazards. I kept remembering my mother, brothers, nephews, and nieces. I may never see them again.

What will happen to me now? Although I was not able to foresee the specific events of a doomsday scenario, I was not optimistic about my future. I was to face the future the way it was destined for me.

The aim of this book is to transmit knowledge about a typical sojourn in a foreign land that was settled by adventurous Europeans. They used brute force and cruelty to subjugate the native inhabitants.

With Bible in one hand and a gun in the other, the immigrants of that era justified their plunder, sexual assault, and slaughter of the natives across the continent as their manifest destiny. They claimed that it was God's plan to replace the indigenous people with White Christians.

Then the skillful immigrants arrived and built this land into a modern nation-state. I began to visualize a picture of uncertainty at every step of my mental landscape. How will I fit in such a challenging society? Perhaps, in time, I would learn to cope with the mishaps and end up belonging here.

Aside the privileged context of inherited status, wealth, and power in which a non-Western student as myself was brought up, there was no guarantee of a smooth progress toward higher education in an alien environment. We were only assured that social acceptance of foreign students in North America had improved. We were tolerated if we followed a narrow path, remained focused on our studies, and went home after our degrees were completed. For a people who are adaptive, willing to work hard, and stay on course, America offered the best that humankind has created. Given my determination and the invisible hand of divine intervention, there was no likely hurdle that could have catapulted my final goal. Thanks to the "angels" that come to the rescue of the underdogs—all is well that ends well!

I

After an overnight stop in London, England, I took an Air Canada flight reaching Toronto after twelve hours in the air. It was an exhausting journey. There was not another passenger from India on this plane, not even actress Nutan Samarth, who was a sojourner on my plane from Mumbai to London. I surmise that she stayed back in London with her relatives. In those days there were very few Indians who travelled to North America.

After passing through immigration and customs at the Toronto International Airport, I collected my suitcase and located the exit sign. Before I could take even one step, I was met by Professor David Pupier, who spotted me as the only probable person arriving from India. He was expecting me. He introduced himself, took my suitcase, and asked me to follow him. He would drive me to my destination about seventy kilometers from Toronto Pearson International Airport. I remember how recklessly he drove his car; he assured me that they drive fast (say one hundred miles per hour) because the roads are only for the motor vehicles. "Cows, bullock carts, and pedestrians are not allowed as in India," he emphasized. "It is different here than India," he chuckled. Since I was awfully tired, I did not respond to his prank.

In less than an hour we arrived at a YMCA where he checked me in and said goodbye. Dr. Pupier was a classmate of my Allahabad Institute boss while they were students at Ithaca, New York. Dr. Jatin Bret Chandran (JBC) helped Pupier visit Jaunpur in Uttar Pradesh,

India, to gather his PhD dissertation data. Jaunpur is about fifteen miles from my hometown.

Entering my YMCA room and seeing a bed, the only possible action for me to take was to lie down. I was dead tired. It seemed I slept for an eternity! When I finally woke, I was utterly confused. For a moment I did not know where I was. It seemed like a thoroughly alien place. I felt as if I had been plucked from one side of the globe and dumped in a bizarre land mass where everything was unfamiliar and peculiar. Suddenly, I became panicky and was overcome with grief. Despair consumed me. *What have I done to myself?* In New Delhi I had friends, relatives, a secure job, stability, and joy in my life. I had people in India who loved me. Here I was alone and felt miserable.

Now, I needed to figure out how to make the best of a presumably bad decision in undertaking this trip to Canada. I took a shower, dressed, and went down to the lobby and looked around. Exiting the lobby, I walked around the building a few times, trying to get a feel for the place. Experiencing hunger, I entered a sort of hole in the wall, where they appeared to be serving only snack food. The cheapest item I saw was potato patties with tomato sauce. Would it taste like the ones I had eaten in a Connaught Place eatery? Could it have been beef patties?

A few hours later, Dr. Pupier came, had me pay for the room, and took me to the campus along with my luggage. There he dropped me off at the prearranged boarding house that was within walking distance to campus buildings. The small upstairs rental room belonged to a widow who charged me twenty-five dollars per month. My food was to be taken at the campus cafeteria. After a week of brooding and hurtling depression, I admitted to Dr. Pupier that I didn't like the place. It was not a locale I had anticipated. If I had had a return airline ticket, I would have gone back home. He recognized my anxiety as a severe case of culture shock. He assured me, "Don't worry. That was how I felt when I arrived in India the first time." That statement, luring as it indubitably was, tended to console me. Why did someone not warn me about this syndrome? As time passed, I began to relax and accept things as they were in my new abode.

After two weeks, Dr. Pupier and his wife arranged a day's outing for me to see Niagara Falls, a natural attraction located about fifty miles from the campus. The Niagara River flows over Niagara Falls at a horseshoe location, creating a forceful spectacle of waterfall, which attracts millions of tourists like me each year. It was an awesome natural attraction I could have never imagined existed.

The trip to Niagara Falls helped to calm my restlessness, and within a week I began to meet other South Asians on campus. One was an instructor in the physics department, and another was an engineering student. Both were from Maharashtra. Two students from Sri Lanka, one Sinhalese and the other a Tamil, were also new to campus. I met them all. Hindu Tamils and Buddhist Sinhalese literally detested each other in Sri Lanka and even in Canada. These two fellows were not comfortable in each other's company, to say the least. The Tamil student continued coming to our cooking sessions. We never saw the Sinhalese fellow again.

The Tamil Ceylonese and the three of us from India secured permission from the dean to use a vacant dormitory room for Indian cooking on weekends once or twice a month.

None of us had ever cooked before. The first time we made chickpea soup or dal, we only used salt and pepper—no spices—and it was inedible. We enjoyed eating the rice though! We decided to look for an Indian restaurant in the area. There was none. Our next challenge was to do research and find a simple recipe. But where would we get the spices? Luckily, there was one Armenian store downtown that carried imported curry powder from England. That would suffice, we agreed.

Once the classes began at the end of September, I got in the flow of things and immediately became engrossed in studies. Catching up was a big challenge because the subjects were thrown at us in rapid succession, week-after-week. In no time, I fell into a routine and became engrossed in studies and completing homework on time. It was unlike anything

I had faced in Indian colleges. There was no time now to think about home and loneliness.

Senior faculty members were cordial and helpful. Being of English ancestry they were familiar with Indian students and their likes and dislikes. In fact, many went out of their way to make us feel welcome. They were my guardian angels. I adored them.

The place where I would be living for several months was in the southwestern region of Ontario, Canada. Known as the Royal City, it was the seat of Wellington County. Because of its low crime rate, clean environment, and relatively high standard of living, it was consistently rated as one of Canada's most livable cities. Located here was a noted agriculture college that was affiliated with the University of Toronto (UT).

UT was a public research university in Ontario province, Canada. This university was founded by a royal charter in 1827 as King's College, and the first institution of higher learning in the colony of Upper Canada. Originally controlled by the Church of England, it was renamed in 1850 upon becoming a secular institution. It consisted of twelve colleges that differed in character and history.

The campus where I was enrolled as a graduate student has undergone a transformation since I graduated from it in 1959. Now a full-fledged university, it is one of Canada's top comprehensive institutions of higher learning with emphasis on basic research. It is a medium-sized institution of higher learning and while it offers degrees in numerous disciplines, it is now acclaimed for its focus on food sciences.

The late John Kenneth Galbraith, Harvard economist and former Ambassador to India, was an alumnus of this famed college. During John F. Kennedy's presidency, Ambassador Galbraith befriended the Nehru family and did bring the two countries much closer. I met Professor Galbraith at a conference on the University of California Berkeley campus in 1988 and we had a tête-à-tête about India and Canada.

When I was a student there, the department of political economy was in two buildings. After the first year, I was assigned an office in the building which is now occupied by the Department of Food, Agricultural, and Resource Economics (FARE). It is the most research-intensive department of its kind in Canada. FARE adopted its new name after I left the campus. It reflects the department's mission and composition more accurately. Originated there was a typical Canadian approach to resource pedagogy. The FARE utilized rigorous tools of statistical analysis to study applied problems in the general area of agricultural trade, food demand analysis, food safety, and biotechnology, along with the economics of renewable resources and the environmental policy. Since the FARE group is interdisciplinary, faculty members actively collaborated with other social scientists through both formal and informal networks.

For developing countries such as India, where there was food scarcity, it was necessary for students like me to be trained in modern agricultural production methods to help the country become self-sufficient. The focus of our training was on policy issues, agri-business, and marketing. My mentors in India were sure that I would be an asset to the bourgeoning field of economic development.

After I graduated with a master's degree in 1959, my former department initiated graduate programs leading to a PhD, emphasizing a curriculum encompassing natural resources, the environment, food economics, and agricultural marketing. In the old British system that would be the subject matter for political economy. If I had stayed in Canada, I would have enrolled for a doctorate degree.

The educational systems in Canada were in sharp contrast to those in India, where I graduated with a Baccalaureate degree. In Canada, the students were exposed to a set of courses that deepened the specialized content of the subject matter.

In India, we took the final examinations at the end of the academic year. In Canada, there was a quarter set-up which meant that the academic year was broken into three terms. We studied a subject for three months and took the final examination at the end of that period. Then we moved on to other subjects.

During 1957-58, I completed five courses that included Calculus,

Principles of Economics, Advanced Farm Management, Agricultural Policies, and Statistical Methods. The latter was offered by the Physics Department. The instructors there were not known to be good communicators; my advisor later saw no reason for that course so early in my graduate education.

Most instructors spoke slowly and in Canadian English. Recently arrived immigrants from Britain, Germany, Hungary, and India were new to Canadian English. We found local diction hard to understand. Almost all professors were educated in American universities. My adviser, Professor Phillip C. Whitman, was a graduate student at a university in the State of Michigan, working on his PhD dissertation.

In preparation for my master's thesis, Professor Whitman guided me step by step. The topic ascertained for my thesis was a study of the capital needs of the low-income family farms. A research design was developed to collect field data using a stratified sample of thirty-four family farms of the lower one-third group of the farm cooperators selected from southwestern Ontario. This sample was purposively selected out of a universe of about four-hundred farmers in Ontario, who during 1957-58, kept their farm records in the cooperative farm accounting project of the department. The farm operations were broken into four categories: Beef-hog, 32.5 percent; Dairy-General, 26.5 percent; Dairy-Specialty; 26.5 percent, and Cash Crop, 14.5 percent.

Professor Whitman, a delightful mentor, was a laid-back, cool-headed scholar. Before the first summer break (June-August), he called me to his office and described my assignment for the summer. He had a list of farms in Ontario province that he wanted me to visit and collect data about their farm operations using a questionnaire. That was my first exposure to field research. I was to be paid five-hundred dollars per month. Having procured a Canadian driver's license, he arranged an official car and gave me maps saying, "now go and talk to those farmers." That was putting a lot of trust in me. Others would have hesitated to ask a foreign student who had been in the country for few months to take charge of a university car and drive around rural areas, visiting and asking sensitive questions of gentlemen farmers, who I had never met. However, these farmers had received a letter from Professor Whitman introducing me and informing them that I would be visiting them that summer.

The central and western regions of Ontario province comprised part of the southern and western Ottawa Huron region that was also known as the St. Lawrence Lowlands. In this area the soil was glacial till of various kinds, under laid by sedimentary rocks. Toward the East there was a much higher proportion of acidic soil.

That summer, I travelled to fifteen counties where the selected family farms were located. The farthest county was Essex and the nearest was Waterloo, followed by Dufferin, Brant, and Wentworth, all nearby. Three to four times a week, I was driving around the countryside. Each day, I tried to visit two to three farms. Over the eight-week period I collected extensive data from thirty-four farmers. These farmers traced their origin to the British Isles. Indeed, Ontario was inhabited predominantly by English migrants. One way or the other, many were connected to India either as members of the civil and armed services or as missionaries.

I met one missionary family that was outgoing, and while serving tea and biscuits the lady insisted that I go to America and study theology. I had no idea as to what that meant. She wanted me to meet her grown-up daughter, but I could not stay long enough to do so.

One day while driving around rural Ontario and visiting farms, I saw on the side of a red barn an inscription: *Seek first his kingdom and his righteousness, and all things will be given to you as well* (Matt. 6:33 NIV). I had to stop for several minutes for meditation. Later, I asked the owner of that barn about the meaning of that idiom. He explained that it was taken from a passage in the Bible in which a promise was being made that if we, human beings, seek God first, and become a decent moral human being, all the earthly desires will become ours. The owner of that barn was pleased that I liked the biblical passage on the side of his barn. He was a devoted Christian.

Indeed, the human condition demands that we seek the grace of God. However, it is not necessary that we become a zealous devotee first.

Devotion to God must be the first in our priority of things to do. Other missionary farmers also told me that you must, *Love the Lord your God with all your soul and your mind* (Matt. 22:37 NIV). God blesses those who are in the Kingdom. Our sins are forgiven in His name. That was a heavy and profound lesson for me. I felt certain that there must be a comparable track in the holy Gita as well. And there was! Indeed, the essence of all religious teachings is the abundance of grace that is at our disposal no matter what.

One of the neighbors where this barn was located invited me for tea several times and chatted extensively about God the savior. Apparently, I reminded him of his missionary relative who spent thirty years in north India. They were also sponsoring a young Indian Christian girl who was studying at Toronto University. They began to write post cards every week and invited me for dinner on many Sundays. They became very protective of me and established an enduring friendship that lasted into the late 1960's when they passed away.

I remember a baffling situation when I met a younger farmer that summer. I located the address of his farm and parked along the road where he was tending to his chores. When I came out of the car and introduced myself, I mentioned Professor Whitman's letter from the nearby college. He said, "Oh! I thought you were someone else. I was expecting an Indian embassy official."

Then he changed the subject and declared, "You know, I have concluded that matrimonial plans between Indians and Canadians do not work out." I was offended and stated, "Sorry, I have no idea about what I am listening. I am here as a student to talk to you about your farm operations."

Then, it was all business and as we chatted about his farm we walked toward his house and spent another hour writing his answers on the questionnaire. Soon thereafter, the lady of the house drove up. She apologized for not being there before and quickly prepared tea and offered fancy biscuits. Canadians drank a lot of tea and used crème and sugar as we did. I reckon it is the British thing. So, I got along well.

Canadians in general have a symbiotic relationship with India. I felt at ease with all the farmers I met. As I was leaving, Mrs. Mason muttered, "I wish (inaudible) was here, she would have loved to talk to you." I said goodbye to them and thanked them profusely for their hospitality. I was sure I made another friend to add to my long list of well-wishers.

Finally, the data collection was completed. I was relieved that I had a successful field work and did not cause any scratches on the official car. In India I drove only jeeps. That summer, I learned far more from the practitioners of food production on these fertile farms than I did in many of the classrooms. Then, I sat down with Professor Whitman and poured over the sheets of data. On the last day of our meeting, there was a knock at the door and when Professor Whitman opened it, he greeted one of the farmers I had interviewed—the one who mistook me to be from Indian High Commission. I recognized him and we exchanged pleasantries. He was with a young woman who was either his sister or daughter. Probably she was the one who I would have met at the farm on the day of my visit. The gentleman was there to consult with the professor about the economies of scale and the possibility of expanding his farm operations. Since I did not have to be there because of the personal financial matters they were to discuss, I excused myself. Professor Whitman told me that he will see me in my student office after a while.

After forty-five minutes, Professor Whitman took all of us for lunch to the campus cafeteria where we ate and chatted. After the professor and his client went back to the office, the farmer's sister and I stayed and talked for close to an hour. I learned part of the story from her about the statement her brother had made to me on the farm regarding matrimony. As it turned out, she worked as a dispatcher at the Indian High Commission in Ottawa and had been engaged to marry a young Indian foreign service employee. He was abruptly transferred by the Ministry of Foreign Affairs, Government of India, to Kampala, Uganda. He left a message for his fiancé that if he continued his alliance, he might lose his job. It appeared that because of the sensitive nature of his

Foreign Service post he was ineffectual in carrying through his liaison. I thought, wow, I was beginning to learn a lot about non-academic subjects as well here in Canada.

By the end of my first year at this college in Canada, I had finished two-thirds of my required course work. Everything began to look doable. Therefore, the second year was dedicated to finishing the remaining course work, analyzing the data, interpreting it for trends, and making charts along with tables. Composition and the final narrative resulted in a 146-page long master's thesis. Now that I had accomplished all the requirements for my MA degree I began to plan for the future.

Because the summer break was long, almost four months, not only did I have an opportunity to see the countryside but the field work for my thesis gave me ample time to learn about Canada and its people. I also followed the popular culture of buying an old car from a graduating student. Now, I became a bit mobile as well. But there was neither an opportunity to drive long distance, nor time at my disposal. All my driving was local and on weekends.

***

Canada occupies a large geographical region of North America, extending from the Atlantic Ocean in the east to the Pacific Ocean on the west, and northward into the Arctic Ocean. By total area, it is the world's second largest country which shares land borders with the United States to the south and northwest.

This portion of North America was the main front during the War of 1812 between the United States and the British Empire. When I lived there, Canada appeared to be sparsely populated and it needed more people to inhabit the land. After the initial period of British and French colonization, four major waves of migration and settlement of non-aboriginal peoples took place over a period of almost two centuries. The British and Irish immigrants were encouraged by the colonial Governors to settle in Canada after the War. These immigrants were mostly British army regulars who had served in that war. The authorities rushed their settlement because they were worried about another American invasion.

To counter the French-speaking influence of Quebec, English Canada accelerated its new settlement mostly into the Ontario province. The Irish immigration to Canada peaked when the Irish Potato Famine occurred. By 1913, another wave of migration took place mostly from continental Europe. Then, a major arrival of more than a quarter million took place in 1957, the same year I arrived. Now there were substantial non-English and non-French speaking populations. This increase included the largest Ukrainian immigrants.

Another source of new citizens was the American rebels from the south who did not want to sever their association with the English royalty. They migrated north into Canada earning the name of loyalists. They were Americans who remained faithful to the British monarchy during the American Revolution! Referred to as Tories, Royalists, or King's Men by the American patriots, it was safer for them to migrate.

Many loyalists, having endured destitution at the hands of the patriots, fled the country, arriving in Britain or Canada. Others settled in the British West Indies, i.e., the Bahamas. Americans of largely Caribbean background fled the United States to escape persecution. Many left the United States during and after the Revolutionary War and settled throughout Canada.

For obvious reasons, it was easier for people like us from India, also a member of the British Dominion, to travel to Canada rather than the U.S. largely because of our familiarity with the British Empire. Also, we were told that America was like a frontier country where that society had not yet reached a stage of civility that would enable her to accommodate diverse kinds of people as Canada had. Lamentably, more than half a century later that syndrome continues.

Canada was also inhabited for millennia by various aboriginal people. Beginning in the late fifteenth century, British and French expeditions explored and later settled the Atlantic coast. In 1763, France ceded nearly all its colonies in North America after the Seven Years' War. In 1867, the British North American colonies formed a Confederation. At the same time, Canada became a federal dominion of four provinces. Thus, began the accretion of additional provinces and territories. Certainly, it allowed a process of increasing autonomy from the United Kingdom. Eventually, the 1931 Statute of Westminster gave rise to the Canada Act of 1982, which helped sever the legal subordination of Canada from the British parliament.

Even to us, the transients, it was apparent that the Canadians in general did not like the domineering American influence. However, they had no choice because they depended on major industries based in the United States—the automobile being the main case in point. There was a perceived love and hate relationship between the two. All my professors, for example, were educated at American universities. That prompted me, just like them, to look southward to the United States for higher education.

***

Once acclimatized to campus routine I was able to manage my time well. Being a small college campus with agronomic foci there were no planned social activities for foreign students. We were there for studies and that is just what we did. Yet we socialized amongst ourselves, South Asians, and West Europeans, to a great extent. East Europeans were a strange bunch; being victims of inferiority complex.

Except for occasional trips to downtown Toronto, we were confined to this virtually quiet college town. Luckily, I had a summer travelling job and that kept me from getting thoroughly bored. Moreover, for us, the non-Europeans, winter was very harsh because it snowed much of the time. The summer was like India's winter season. Routinely, we went from one building to the other—from our rooms to our offices, to the cafeteria, to classrooms, and back to our offices to study. One day as I sat down in the cafeteria with my food tray, I was joined by Professor Pupier, the person who brought me from the airport. He looked at my plate and asked me, "What do you think you are eating?" "Vegetarian patty," I answered. He laughed and told me I was eating pork. Shocked, I turned around to stare at the cook and with a big sigh I muttered, "Well, sooner or later it was bound to happen." For these East European Neanderthal cooks, I averred, "The mixed vegetables with meat made the dish a vegetarian meal!"

Often, we would meet Canadian foreign civil servants stationed in New Delhi. One day, I met a gentleman who came to campus and chatted with me for a while. We talked about his work in India and when he was leaving, he revealed, "They like you here and your country likes me there. So, I am going back to my job in Delhi." I did not envy him at all. By now, I was deeply buried in my studies. I too was getting used to Canada.

One day while studying in my graduate office, I received a phone call from the lady I had met in Professor Whitman's office and had lunch with about two months earlier. I recalled a rather personal conversation with her in the cafeteria then. She said she was passing through and would want to stop by. I said certainly, please do so. When she arrived, she took me to a downtown cafeteria for tea. We introduced ourselves informally and began our friendship. Lyz Mason told me she had been to Kitchener, a nearby town, for an interview at a bank. She might be moving away from Ottawa and will be closer to her family in southwestern Ontario. She seemed happier than she had been before. She promised she would call when she finds a place to live in Kitchener. I wished her luck and said a warm goodbye.

There was an assortment of foreign students in the department; three from the United Kingdom including a slightly older man from Scotland, a German, and two Hungarians. One of the latter was an arrogant asshole but his wife was a real sweet lady. Employed as a secretary in the department, she typed a rough draft of my thesis. The Englishmen, having had the colonial upbringing felt they were superior to others, but their grades did not support that claim. It must have been embarrassing for them to get B's and C's. Therefore, from the very beginning they became much humbler toward us. The younger English fellow was a happy go lucky type, nothing bothered him. The younger Hungarian fellow was unpretentious, gentle but particularly meek. He insisted that I meet his dad, a new immigrant, who had a house in the neighboring county. The student from Germany was stern. Once he and I had an intense discussion on the divisions of nation-states—East Germany and West Germany, India and Pakistan. I asked him about the possibility of German unification. He assured me that it would never happen. He retorted, "Will India and Pakistan ever become one country again?" I likewise answered, "Never." Then we both laughed. The former merged, the latter did not, and never will!

The professors in the department were exceedingly pleasant and helpful, except for the fellow who brought me from the airport. He was supercilious and not liked by the staff. He was known to be unscrupulous. He was nice to me though. When I had initially arrived on campus, a senior professor who worked in British India made sure I was comfortably situated in the room I rented, and that my office where we did most of our studies was fully furnished.

During my second year of study abroad, my mentor from Allahabad, Dr. JBC, was at Ithaca New York, where he was preparing to submit his PhD dissertation. He asked me to visit him. I prevailed upon the Indian instructor in physics department, a member of our weekend cooking group, to drive his car to New York. We stopped in Ithaca, met my former boss, and then drove on to New York City for sightseeing.

Having worked during the summer months, I began to feel economically secure and, as mentioned previously, I was also a proud owner of an Oldsmobile that reminded me of my father's Oldsmobile he had purchased in 1946. I learned driving using his car with the help of his chauffeur.

The first time I drove my car downtown it had snowed the night before. I was a bit nervous. All graduate students living off-campus needed a car to drive to campus. The Anglos needed it for dating purposes. Out of four men from India, three of us had a car. Unlike the

Anglos, we had no social use for it. It was just parked, with occasional drives to downtown, about two miles downhill.

My only significant outings were when I was invited by the local churches and social clubs to give a talk on India. Usually, it was a dinner program and as a standard practice they wanted to have an exotic person from a faraway land to become a showpiece for an hour. In addition to free food, I would invariably meet either retired missionaries to India, or ex-soldiers who were in India during World War II.

It was after one of those presentations on India, the excerpt of which was published in the local newspaper, that I received a very disapproving letter from a former missionary to India. He was working at a local Church of Our Lady Immaculate. I remember the name of his church because I had to look up the meaning of immaculate (spotless, perfect, flawless). His letter was far from it.

He congratulated me by declaring that of all the people from India he had met, he thought I communicated very well. He then picked portions of my talk and accused me of propagandizing about Hinduism. To him Hinduism was an unrefined and primitive religion. I now wish I had saved that letter to show to people how narrow-minded, pompous, messy, and misguided this missionary was. No wonder many missionaries in India were known as colonial agents of the British first, and people of God second. Intermittently, they became greedy political meddlers. Obviously, there are phony Christians as distinguished from the pious Christians.

As the Canadian winter arrived the days were getting shorter, and we began to feel gloomy. We hankered for a change. Something cheerful was most welcome. Before long I heard the good news from Lyz Mason who had not only secured a job at a bank in Kitchener but had rented a suitable apartment where she was to move during the coming weekend. Therefore, she asked me if I could come over and help her move. I was more than eager to accept her invitation. I arrived at her new apartment by noon on that Saturday. The apartment was partially furnished but Lyz wanted to change few things. Some of her belongings were still at her family farm about eighteen miles away. Her brother brought over a sofa, a table, and two chairs in his truck. The rest we hauled in one trip using both of our cars.

That is when the hard work began because the challenge was to accommodate everything in a one-bedroom apartment. But first the whole place had to be cleaned. This was something I had never done before. So, I was mostly an onlooker but did help move the heavy stuff that I was asked to do. The immediate goal was to place the sofa at one end so it could face the television. In fact, we watched TV as we took a little break after moving the heavy coffee table. We had brought a picnic basket from the farm which we placed on the coffee table along with a case of Canadian Molson and two glasses. After we finished arranging the heavy furniture, it was dinner time. Thus, we toasted the move with a glass of another Molson and ate supper. Then we drank some hot tea as the TV blasted away. Although, I drank a little of Molson followed by a glass of ginger ale in those days, I did not know how much I had consumed that evening. I must have dozed off and when I woke up my left cheek was resting on Lyz's left breast. I was embarrassed but Lyz smiled in approval. We talked some more and began to yawn. By now we were both tired and so we went to sleep.

We were not in a hurry to get up early. After late breakfast, we stayed in gloriously tranquil mood all day. No doubt our inner goddess was still basking in the aftermath of a celestial glow. I did not want to leave and wished to stay on indefinitely. But I had early morning classes on Monday, and of course Lyz had to go to work at the bank on Monday morning. After putting away the remaining household items and rearranging few items I left Kitchener on that Sunday evening. I had a great time. *What an alluring country? I like it here*, I muttered to myself. I felt I would be returning to that abode soon.

During the second year of my studies in Canada, I completed five more courses: Advanced Economic Theory, Price and Index Analysis, Marketing Agricultural Products, Advanced Research Methods, and Rural Sociology. In addition, I finalized my master's thesis entitled,

A Study of the Capital Needs of the Low-Income Family Farms in Southwestern Ontario.

***

The twentieth month of my stay in Canada was approaching and as expected, pressures began to build on many fronts, private and public, that challenged my disposition. My personal life had one prearranged route that was on track. It was a fact that there was no immediate sign of my returning to Delhi. Even in the Arthaśāstra it is written that if a companion has gone abroad and is not heard of, his partner shall wait for him for only seven menstrual cycles. I had been absent for a much longer duration and a definite plan of action was stipulated under such eventuality. To put that to rest, I was notified with a document and the matter was settled.

Similarly, I began to hear from my former employers at the Indian Cooperative Union in Delhi and Dr. JBC from Allahabad. In addition, my eldest brother inquired about my plans for returning to India. Simultaneously, my department head had sent me to a pre-arranged meeting with the local immigration officer. Something even more intriguing was to happen. I was being prepared to stay on.

There was an Indian student from Guyana who socially mingled with us. During a casual conversation about his family, he mentioned his uncle Dr. Joy Cherrian. I perked up. During 1954-55, when I was a journalism student in Nagpur, India, I was assigned to follow up on the visit of Dr. Cherrian and Mr. Ben Burnham, leaders of People's Progressive Party (PPP) in British Guyana. They were on a fact-finding mission to India and were seeking India's support for their country's impending freedom from the British rule. Both had fallen ill. When I went to their hotel on the second day of their stay, they were still convalescing. So, I brought a physician who examined them and prescribed needed medicines. They soon recovered and I got to know them well.

When that student from Guyana went home during Christmas time, he borrowed my camera. While visiting his uncle he mentioned about me and his uncle remembered his days with me in India. During the week, his nephew was visiting him he had become a member of the government. Thereupon, I wrote a letter congratulating him. I was surprised that he replied promptly, asking me to keep in touch.

As my stay in Canada was coming to an end, a series of correspondence were received. The gist of those conveys the story about my future. What follows is to recast the various lead-ins for me that would require prompt actions.

The first letter came from the Indian Cooperative Union's Development and Research Center that had granted me a twenty-month leave of absence, effective 21st September 1957. I had fifty-one days of earned leave to my credit there and the rest of the leave was to be treated as study leave without pay. The Deputy Director of the Rural Development Division of this organization reminded me that my leave of absence expired on 1st of May 1959. They were expecting that I would join them again and would be grateful if I could inform them about my plans.

In the above letter nothing specific was included that could have possibly enticed me, i.e., a new assignment and promotion. Lacking any interest, I totally ignored that letter. I did not consider their letter either sincere or of valid concern. If it had impressed me, given the choices at hand, I might have responded.

A second letter came from Georgetown, Guyana. Not surprisingly, this letter was from Dr. Joy Cherrian, Minister of Trade and Industry. Guyana was on its way to achieving independence from the British. Five of his colleagues were participating in the Government, but with extremely limited powers. To paraphrase Dr. Cherrian, the main portfolios were still in the hands of the British officials and the Governor still had the veto powers. The Constitutional stance was somewhat like that of India in 1935. They were continuing their agitation to secure self-government for the country. The Legislative Council that year unanimously passed a resolution calling on the British authorities to grant self-government to Guyana. Unfortunately, the Colonial Secretary in London had side-tracked that resolution and was about to set up a committee to consider how much constitutional advance Guyana should have. This was a usual delaying tactic to which all of them were opposed and they were now carrying out a vigorous campaign against that.

I must reiterate that when I, as a journalism student, was with Joy Cherrian on his fact-finding visit to Nagpur, we had discussed the British tactics in India and especially the role youth like me had innocently played in various protest marches and agitations against the British presence in every nook and cranny of our society. Therefore, I thought it was natural that Cherrian was sharing his anxieties with respect to fighting for his country's independence.

Guyana is bordered on the east by Suriname, on the south and southwest by Brazil, on the west by Venezuela, and on the north by the Atlantic Ocean. It was discovered by Europeans in 1498. The Spanish, French, Dutch, and British quarreled for centuries to occupy that land. Originally a Dutch colony in the seventeenth century, Guyana became a British possession by 1815. The abolition of slavery led to a shortage of free labor for the colonizers. Hence, they imported indentured laborers from India to work on the British owned sugar plantations. Among its population, close to half were followers of Hinduism. The rest could trace their origin to southern Africa. As is the colonial modus operandi, the ethno-cultural division was bound to create a turbulent discord between the two contending citizens.

In January of 1959, I received another letter from Dr. Cherrian. He informed me that recently a post for an agricultural economist was advertised. He was not sure whether the post had already been filled. However, if this had not been done, he felt sure that I would have a good chance with my qualifications in filling that post. He promised to inform me later what the position was.

Later, an appointment letter for that post arrived. A bulky package containing the official documents was sent by the Public Service commission, Government of Guyana. Truly, as eager as I was to accept that offer, something inside me said that I should not go there. There were three reasons that I did not want to take the route of accepting a civil service job in Guyana. One, my obligation was primarily to be of service to the villages of India with which I was most familiar and had been groomed for. Second, I was hesitant to face the British rule in a colony that was being ruthlessly governed. I had experienced that while growing up in India, and I would probably have exceeded the limits of my tolerance in a British colony. Third, a fundamental choice was to seek admission in an American university to pursue doctorate degree before looking for a job in a Third World country. It was very tough for me at that point to write to Dr. Joy Cherrian about my decision not to come to his country. But he understood and encouraged me in my pursuit for higher education in the United States of America. He had earned his own doctorate at Chicago.

As I had been exploring my future after earning my master's degree in Canada, I sought out advice from an especially important person, Dr. JBC, my mentor and former employer at Allahabad Institute. In his letter of January 27, 1959, he wrote:

> Regarding your future, you have stated three possibilities. Let me comment on them. If you are set on completing your PhD and can meet all the financial obligations, it might be worth going ahead with further graduate work in the United States of America. The disadvantage in this course of action is that you will be away for a long time from your country and, as such, be in danger of becoming a back number and a misfit.
>
> Let us face facts and be honest with ourselves. You really have two alternatives. One is to remain in the United States indefinitely and perhaps take up citizenship. The second alternative is to return to India. Do not expect to get a job or secure a position in India before you leave there, or even within a few weeks of your arrival in India.

The longer you stay away from your country the more difficult you will find it to adjust. I would, therefore, suggest that you, firstly, be quite honest with yourself about what you want to do with your life. Many things are happening, great changes are taking place. You will be wise to become a part of these changes and fortified with specialized training, you can make a worthy contribution to the program of development.

JBC's letter was direct and candid. The straight-forward content of his letter began to open my eyes regarding future plans on my part. It made me face reality. If nothing else, I had to be honest in truly examining my alternatives. His advice based on his own experience was in a way very disheartening. All that hullabaloo and emphasis on foreign education for Indian youth did not mean much after all. In any case, his exposé was instrumental in helping me decide upon pursuing a PhD degree. I began to direct my focus on further seeking admission for graduate studies in the United States of America. Consequently, I began to write letters of inquiry to chosen American universities for admission and financial assistance. Then, unexpectedly, two months later I received another letter from Allahabad's JBC the content of which surprised me.

You will be finishing your master's degree this June, I believe. When do you propose to return? I am anxious to know since there is an opening in a proposed scheme for expansion of Extension Training endeavors at the Institute. I write to enquire when you can be available. Will you please reply as soon as possible?

Quite a heartening letter it was because the doomsday scenario alluded to in his previous letter that returning students to India face, as to uncertainty about employment, was somewhat negated in this letter.

I thought that surely the situation must be changing. By this time, I was well advanced in my pursuit of a placement at an American university. Now I was torn between the two alternatives at hand. I was curious about the remuneration. Hence, I wrote to JBC indicating my interest in the position. His reply came promptly, within three weeks.

> I was glad to receive your letter of May 12th and to know that you are interested in the possible opening in the proposed scheme of Extension Training. Here are some of the details. The Extension Directorate of the Ministry of Food and Agriculture is planning to establish four institutes of Extension Education in India.
>
> The purpose is to provide training to all instructors of the Extension Training Centers in India through a three-month refresher course in extension education and related subjects. Three such courses are to be offered each year by each of the designated institutions.
>
> There are six senior posts at each institute, one of which is in the field of your expertise. The salary is rupees 350 – 850 range. It is for this post that I have you in mind as a possible candidate.
>
> Please keep me informed about your travel plans so that I would know where to contact you.

Wow! It was quite a letter of encouragement. It is possible I could get a job in India with my graduate education abroad. I could possibly secure it while still living outside India. But I noted no definite promise of any kind in the job prospect. Everything was quite tentative. The salary was particularly low. I worked at the same Institute during 1954-1956 and was paid twice the amount quoted above.

I discussed this letter with my graduate adviser and local mentor, Professor Phillip Whitman, and straight away he did not think highly of pursuing that job prospect in India because of the tentativeness of the letter's narrative. Instead, Professor Whitman and I discussed the letters that I had received from numerous American universities. There were three categories of letters: (1) letters from universities such as those from Tennessee that were discouraging because of racism, intolerance, and lack of security for students of color; (2) letters from universities that would grant admission to the graduate program but no guarantee of financial assistance, and (3) letters from universities that would offer both admission and financial assistance. Having been a student at a mid-Western university of the United States it was known to Professor Whitman that a major university in the State of Missouri had an exchange program with India's four eastern provinces. He concluded that such a campus would likely be safer for colored students because the community would be familiar with people from India. Surely, they would have seen a few of them around and would not feel threatened!

***

It was during the second year in Canada that I also began to interact with my family in India. My oldest brother served the role of a guardian after the premature death of our father. In a letter he wanted to know the date of my departure from Canada and arrival date in India. But he did not mean to expatiate or dwell upon it provided there were rays of hope about PhD, without which my overseas visit will not be fully justified. At the same time, he thought that if I was fed up with the climate and surroundings it was not worth staying there.

Invariably, in all his letters, my sister-in-law would write something soothing about my predicament. Being a natural healer, she was always concerned about my welfare. She would also inform me about the wellbeing of my mother and brothers.

As mentioned above, the real encouraging influence in those days came from Professor Phillip Whitman, my academic adviser, and my new friend Ms. Lyz Mason whom I consulted regularly and met frequently.

The next letter from India was quite disturbing. It inquired about my progress toward a definite plan to return home. The gist was that if I had stayed in India, I could have financially supported the younger brothers to achieve their goals. The two younger brothers had approached college age at the same time. I sensed the problem was insufficient funds for those pursuing post baccalaureate degrees. Assets generated from the joint family property were not accessible to them. That, therefore, had caused a major family crisis. I was told that the brother younger to me had to postpone his ambition for completing his MA degree. Then, the next younger brother had to drop his idea of continuing his education for a PhD degree. After that litany, my older brother's storyline turned snappy.

> As per your indications given in your last letter it seems that you have completed your education, but you have not conveyed result of your endeavors. It seems that you have taken up employment for four months. Everything is good but all in your interest. You are not caring to think about the interests and ambitions of other brothers which I must do. I know instances where people go to foreign countries; they earn, they study, and support members at home. I do not understand specialty in your case.

This letter was uncharacteristically full of innuendos, and I became ever more annoyed as I continued reading it to the end. He had more damaging thoughts to get across.

> During mother's trip to this place, she expressed that people are taunting that after the death of our father, grown-up boys in the family are not being married and, indirectly, I am being blamed for all these. I do not mean to discourage you but want you to think about

family's financial situation as they stand. Please look
in the interest of all and then decide your future career.

Wow again! Is he suggesting that I postpone my plans? Will I be
able to come back later to North America to continue my education? As
I pondered over the tone of his letter, I became angry and frustrated.
It filled my psyche with utter disappointment. I was appalled at their
gullibility and misjudgment. What should I do? Just thinking about
that letter was distracting me from my studies. I could not shake off
the content of that letter for quite some time. It was taking a lot of
mental space at a time when I was trying to put final touches to my
master's thesis and preparing for the final oral examination. No doubt,
this family quagmire was tossed at me at an inopportune time.

Growing up in this joint knotty family of a village called Pura
Qanoon Goyan, I had experienced that our elders did not actually see
who we were like, but rather as reflections of other people they had heard
about. In psychoanalysis, this notion is called transference. It seems their
brain ran a continuous loop of scary ideas and images. Most of the time
when their minds thought of fictitious paranoid stories, they invented
images as if they were the reality. They forgot that thoughts were not
facts. For them only what they thought constituted absolute truth. Often,
they jumped to the level of their conclusion without knowing the details,
thus processing it at the level of fiction, not the truth!

Youth of my joint family have had visions of breaking out of the
reach of their elders whose established thought patterns were of great
hindrance to their free-thinking adolescences. This was a major source
of contention inwardly where the growing youth saw themselves in
ways that would not meet the approval of the family structure. The
hierarchical authoritarianism that reigned in our extended family
shunned the creative minds of the growing youth. It led to repression
in general, and a lack of support for independent thought and action, in
particular.

We were expected to do those things that preserved the age-old established family tradition. The structure might have been faulty, but nonetheless it was to be maintained. Departing from the established rules could have and did have dire consequences for us. As such, domination was practiced within the family make-up itself. In the end, we were left only to comply. *Do as we say, not as we do*, motto was sickening. Our unhappiness and discontent were absolutely ignored to preserve the uprightness of the illogically harmful family hierarchy.

Did it ever occur to them how the youngsters treated in that foolish way would respond and rebel? How much disrespect they would accumulate from the younger generation? The resilient youth with strong psyche succeeded in putting a distance from their hypocrite elders. Eventually, they escaped from their grasp. Possibly, that sprouted the idea in my instinctive mind that if I had to function on a virtuous path, I would have to discover it myself.

Failure to concentrate on my studies, I thought that composing an appropriate response might explain and bring a closure to this issue of my role in financially relieving the family. However, there was a risk in doing so. Old Indian tradition forbids younger members from "talking back" to their elders. But I took the risk. I had already earned negative points. *What else can they do? Chastise me further?* At least the real facts would eventually seep in, and it could begin to exonerate me to some extent. Such decisions can prove to be liberating, or they can signify a point of no return. Rather than feeling sorry for myself, a month prior to leaving Canada, I composed the following letter so that I would get on with my studies.

My dear respected brother,

Your letter received after a long silence was of concern to me. Inasmuch as, I would abstain from exhibiting irresponsibility, and not cause further confusion, please allow me to express myself. Your last letter, puzzling as it was in comparison with previous ones, showed a marked departure from any preconceived norm. But before I respond, I would request you to take the contents of my letter in a spirit in which it is intended; that is, just to clarify the points raised by you.

There were three stages of my studies here: the course work, the thesis, and oral examination. The first was completed last April 1959, and the second in June. I had my oral quiz on 31st July 1959. That is all. There was nothing definite to convey about my endeavors. I could not possibly write that something definite had been achieved when it was not at that time.

The employment was in the form of stipend in the department in which I have been pursuing studies and was solely meant to pay for my living expenses as it did for other qualified students. This was the only source wherefrom I could get about nine-thousand rupees per year for expenses. Probably, it has not been realized that I had taken a great risk to have left for a foreign country with meager funds to come by. But I had ambitions and worked diligently on my own and have come this far. I do not remember having given any indication that I was indifferent to others' ambitions. The initiative and capabilities of those who have ambition must come in the forefront so that others can understand the genuine need for when it is possible, as is the usual course. In my case, it was not a dream come true until 1957 when I could resume my education about four years after earning a Baccalaureate degree. The personal realization, I think, would always be the endeavor of the individual.

Contrary to your information about someone who earns, studies, and supports members at home, I know at least a dozen students in this college, who get help from home in cash as well as in kind. Do I have any grudges? Or is there any specialty in my case? None, I understand and realize the things as they stand, considering the set-up we have in our extended family. I would be reluctant to think that there should be any promises to make or break. Rather these so-called words comprise our plans and possibilities. They should be our obligations. So are they mine.

Your letter has not discouraged me. On the other hand, it has helped me make my decisions firmer after giving due thought to the things as they stand. Personally, I think it is a choice between things as they are and the way they should be. My future career need not be decided in the interest of all. The interest which you mention is the financial help for younger brothers which shall be done as soon as I am ready.

I do not mean to contradict you, sir, or be a cause of indignation for I sincerely regard your views and understand your burdensome responsibilities. It was but your encouragement and sacrifice that has rendered this possible for me so far, and I have no one in sight other than you to look for moral support, particularly now when I need it. To me this is a most crucial point of decision making in my life. I am going to try something bigger this time and take a greater risk than ever before.

I concurred with a part of his letter in which he had mentioned about PhD, without that it will not be justified my visit to overseas. At the end, he enquired again about my return plan and asked if I had got some good news.

Be that as it may, I also informed him that I had been accepted by an American university for PhD course starting in September 1959. Accordingly, I shall leave Canada soon. Please anticipate, I informed him, hearing from me from the United States about 700 miles southwest from here when I have settled down.

***

Analyzing the situation that my older brothers faced while I was abroad was challenging to say the least. On the one hand, they wished I would complete my higher education, and on the other hand, there was a shortage of earners in the family compared to the college age youngsters in the family. Although the frustrations that were directed at me by them seemed contradictory and therefore confusing, they were reflecting a genuinely felt reality of the family. No doubt, there was a shortage of resources to raise the younger brothers who were stacked up and rapidly coming of age.

In our family of my widowed mother the task of raising six children at home without a steady source of income had become overwhelming. The members of the joint family leaders behaved in cruel, reckless, and harmful ways toward a significant shareholder living few miles away in Gyanpur. They were ignoring my mother's needs and the older brothers had their own families to care for. Hence, I was the logical person who could have assisted in the family expenses. I did that from the day I got my first job in 1954 until the time I left for Canada in 1957. After leaving the nest and availing of the freedom to travel, I was on a path to pursue a profession and abandoning that in the middle was not only senseless, but cowardice, and ill-advised. With that mighty ambition, all familial and patriarchal pressure directed at me was uncalled for.

Our family wealth in the form of land holdings during the leadership of my father's oldest brother in the early 1940s hovered around 2000 acres. Reliable sources have revealed that during the management of my uncle and his descendants, there was purportedly a systematic transfer of titles to a few. Apparently, farmland was allegedly sold without transparency. Incomes thus generated were not distributed to other legal owners of the land in this dysfunctional joint family. It was kept in the village coffers for the use of those in control.

Currently, the total family land holding is an enigma wrapped in mystery. It boggles my mind, and it should enrage everyone for being duped. What my mother faced as a single parent was not supposed to happen in a normally compassionate joint Hindu family. The proceeds from my father's one-third share should have gone to her. If my father had acted in his own self-interest, he could have saved ample funds for his own children. Instead, he acted as the cash cow for the family because as a lawyer in a nearby town he was the main earner in this family. Documents show that he provided cash to his brothers to buy and amass land. Also, he paid for college education for his brother's sons: two of them became lawyers themselves. So, whither joint family propriety? Where was justice? Where was fair play? What happened to the principles of Hindu kindness, not to ask for love and morality? Why was that avenue of funds from joint property not available to my mother? Why it was not sought, fought for and obtained first? After all, that could have been claimed first before jeopardizing my plans for higher education while living abroad.

I had now graduated and earned a master's degree from a major Canadian university. I had sold my car and disposed of unnecessary items that I thought I would be able to acquire later, if needed. Having secured a student visa from the United States Embassy in Toronto, I left Canada for the Midwest during the first week of September 1959. My confidant, Lyz Mason, who spent a day with me helping make final arrangements, took me to the local Greyhound bus station, and I said goodbye to Canada not knowing what lay ahead. But at least it was not as agonizing as when I left India two years earlier.

II

On a brilliant, sun-drenched day, I boarded a Greyhound bus in Ontario, Canada, bound for the Midwest, United States of America. It was to be a long two and a half-day journey. As the bus reached the highway, my thoughts went back to the day when my plane had taken off from Mumbai Airport for London. The intense emotion of leaving my homeland then had absolutely besieged me with emotions, and I had become a total wreck. This journey was different. Yet it was an extension of the one that had begun in 1957.

Even though the bus stopped at many places as required by law, it seemed I was continuously on the road. Also, the bus itself was replaced every twelve hours. During this extended road trip, I had time to take an exhaustive catalog of events in my life so far. I felt impassive and unemotional compared to the time I'd left India. I resolved to put at rest all that I had gone through with my kinfolk during the last months in Canada and to start anew.

Many of us carry memories of our ecstatic good times, past mistakes, hurts, and letdowns of yesterday. Was it possible to erase that and make peace with those who harbored ill feelings by simply accepting them? If not, was it not possible to experience new life and the joy it might bring? Already at my young age (early twenties)—having experienced leaving my homeland and now departing from Canada—I had encountered many people who were stuck in the past. They had become angry and mean-spirited, had little or no self-esteem, and blamed everyone else for their miserable lives. I did not want to be affected by this human drivel; to do so would be a stumbling block to fully experiencing my days as a graduate student in the United States.

Amid the road noise of the bus, many thoughts exuded from my mind as intellectual constructs. How could I apply them to my new life in a new social milieu? It seemed easy to resolve old matters, as what I needed to do was to accept people I met as good in essence. I would not be biased against others.

By the time I arrived at my destination, I was utterly exhausted. A letter from the university's foreign student adviser had directed me to check in at the International House. Upon arrival at the bus station, I hired a taxi to take me to the International House. After entering the lobby, I was told they had no room available for me, so I left my luggage and walked to the Student Housing Office. There, I found I had been assigned a dormitory room in a temporary World War II trailer on campus. Food would be served in the student cafeteria.

Not again, I thought.

After I had moved my luggage from the International House to the dormitory, I was able to finally take a brief nap.

Just before dinner, my roommate showed up, another foreign student, an Iranian. We could have been twin brothers. I wondered how they'd matched us in the absence of algorithm apps then. Instantly, I knew how!

The room began to look very jam-packed. In Canada, I always had my own room. I felt uncomfortably herded here and began to conjure up plans to move out and find a private room. But before that, there were other tasks at hand.

My first errand was to appear before the chairman of the department, who had offered me admission as a graduate student. He assigned me a newly hired faculty adviser, Dr. Rufus Kleinmann, who was waiting for me in his office. Dr. Kleinmann and I talked extensively about my studies in Canada. And based upon that discussion, he came up with a plan for my coursework. He stipulated that the coursework would require four semesters, or two years, and then I would be able to take comprehensive examinations, both written and oral. At the successful completion of those exams, I would write a research dissertation. Although that seemed sometime in the future, I felt I must embark upon my studies right away.

The following morning when I saw him, he took me to the graduate student room, where I was assigned a desk. He also informed me I would serve as his research assistant, working on one of his projects, and would be paid a stipend at the rate of $1,200 per academic year.

The move from Canada to the United States was not as smooth as I'd expected. There were many unknowns. First, I wanted to move out of the crowded dormitory and settle down in a private and suitable accommodation as quickly as possible. So, when classes started, I went to the foreign student adviser and complained about the unsatisfactory living arrangement and the poor quality of food in the cafeteria. He suggested I move off campus and live with other students from India, who might have an apartment or a rental house. He gave me a name to call.

When I dialed that number, a young man by the name of Maniar answered. Maniar said he did have a spare room on the second floor of a house he was renting. Indeed, there was a suitable and a private room for me to move into immediately. It was a lucky break.

In addition to Maniar and myself, there were two others who shared the second floor of the house. Dr. Reddiyar and his younger brother, Gopi, were very compatible. The apartment was centrally located. The A&P grocery store, the student union, the library, classrooms, and my department office were in walking distance.

Arriving here was not like when I'd arrived in Canada two years earlier. I was not homesick here, and there was no culture shock. Now, it felt like business as usual. This was a much larger campus that was not quite as parochial. There were about one hundred foreign students. Even Canadian students were foreigners here.

The university's academic year was divided into two regular

semesters—fall (August to December) and winter (January to May). A summer session (June to July) was optional. I arrived in town before the start of the fall 1959 semester and was enrolled to complete required coursework during the regular semesters, excluding summers. The course of studies I was pursuing was in a standard academic department that functioned as a unit of the Office of Graduate Education. Unlike its counterpart in Canada, it had no stated mission. During the first semester, I was enrolled in four courses—International Finance, Public Policy and Private Enterprise, Farm Business Analysis, and Research— each worth three units of credit.

On the first day of our classes, the instructors distributed a course syllabus listing the topics, textbook assignments, and a research paper. Usually, we were briefed on what subject matter we would study. Most professors came prepared with their lectures, and in fact, one professor started talking as soon as he entered the classroom. It seemed he had memorized the day's lecture and must get it out before a student interrupted and asked a question. Another professor from the same department with a Texas accent should have been a Shakespearean actor; we were so mesmerized by his eloquence that the hour was over before we realized it. Most professors spoke normally and had a measured coverage of the subject for the day.

I was thrilled to be attending classes that were slightly more relaxed and less formal than the Canadian ones. In all these classes, I stood out because of my appearance. In fact, one instructor of German ancestry, who later became a dean, not seeing me in class the first ten minutes one day, asked the class, "Where is that Indian from Canada?" I was amazed and bewildered when I learned about it from my classmates.

When I arrived, I was asked a question on the previous day's lecture. Each instructor had his or her own idiosyncrasies; for instance, in this class, if a student was late or absent, he or she was asked a question.

Usually, we were tested twice in each class—a midterm and a final. Invariably, we had to submit a research paper on a previously approved topic. With the semester format, we were afforded a significant break between the two terms per year. Fall semester was followed by Christmas holidays. The second semester, or spring semester, was followed by a lengthy summer break during June and July. There were summer classes also, but only selected students who had extra funds and wished to graduate earlier enrolled in them. For foreign students, the summer semester was optional. That gave us a chance to work extra and earn money. I also worked on an enhanced basis on the research projects of various instructors who had received outside grants.

There is nothing like a university campus during the summer months. It was peaceful, and we finally belonged to this place. During summer months, most people were not to be seen in town. Except for the foreign students and the stray dogs, the streets were barren, and the stores, empty. Professors who had not left town for fieldwork abroad were holed up either in their offices or in their library cubicles. Noticeably, this town was desolate, to say the least, during the sultry summer.

Having completed all my course requirements at the beginning of summer 1961, I was happy and felt at ease. And as the heat baked everything outside, which I was not prepared for because I had lived in cold Canada, I felt agonizingly short of breath. I had the worst case of hay fever. At times, I gasped for air and felt I would pass out. As a result of a serious episode, I was admitted to the student clinic. Being a foreign student from India who was raised in the tropics, how could it be? The tests revealed I was chronically allergic to ragweed and pollen from oak and maple trees, which were everywhere. The remedy was periodic injection of allergens.

Summer turned into autumn, and when the winter semester began, it brought relief. But before long, the weather turned cold and blizzardy. I was enrolled in research courses only and worked on my adviser's projects. In addition, the time was fast approaching that would compel me to intensify my preparation for the written comprehensive examinations. During the preparation time, I would study for up to seven hours in seclusion in a library cubicle.

Normally, each graduate student was assigned a work and study area in a large room, where there was space for at least six graduate students. However, for serious study, we went to the general library. Each student was at a different level. All of us were assigned a research task, for which we were paid a stipend. In my case, it was now $2,000 per academic year. For the summer months, the stipend was higher, depending on the workload and endowment funds at the disposal of our advisers. Also, I was on Curator's Grant-in-Aid, which paid for my tuition. Since I maintained a high GPA, I was on this grant for the entire period I was a student at this university.

During the 1959-60 academic year, I was on probation. All newcomers were under scrutiny and remained so till they passed the qualifying examination for the PhD program. Largely, it was a function of how well we did in the courses. The department chair, in consultation with a few professors, decided which of the graduate students were worthy of continuing their studies toward their goal. The following year, I was approved for PhD candidacy. I was at ease now. Also, my stipend had been raised to $2,400 per annum. I felt settled.

One of the trends among the senior foreign graduate students was to buy a used automobile and see the local sights and go on picnics with friends, including friends of the opposite gender. I bought an old Chevrolet from a Korean student who was leaving for home after graduation. Then I uncovered a serious problem with the hood. Apparently, on his return from Chicago, the hood of his car had gotten unlatched and had flown backward, bending it badly. Friends pointed out to me that it was not safe to drive that car. So, I returned it to the owner and got my $300 back. What a break!

But the contagion of owning a car of my own, in a good condition, kept nagging until I found an acceptable used Oldsmobile for the same amount. By that time, I had rented a small apartment with a kitchenette on University Avenue, almost next door to my office. In this three-storied building, every occupant was an Indian graduate student, except a sociology student from Pakistan. Chaudhary was a nice guy and very friendly. Mutually, we decided not to display our friendship in public because it was improper for an Indian student to befriend a Pakistani student and vice versa. I was told not to be friendly toward a Pakistani, as it confused the locals! They expected us to be antagonistic toward each other. We acted likewise.

Chaudhary coined a phrase for me, "confident bordering on being cocky!" We used to call each other "buddy boy." We had friends in common, and during the summer months, we began to explore the vicinity.

***

Before the European migrants arrived here, those who inhabited the region were known as the Osage Indians. In 1678, France claimed all this territory. In 1803, the Lewis and Clark Expedition used the Missouri River extensively. Daniel Boone and his sons established, in 1806, a salt mine about forty miles northwest of where the campus was located.

Although this area was full of slave-holding landlords, it was unaffected by the Civil War. The agricultural areas extending all the way to the central part of the state were decidedly proslavery. Without slaves as laborers, there would be no food production. For some reason, this university became a base for the Union troops. But no battles were fought here; the presence of troops discouraged the Confederate guerrillas from attacking, although in nearby towns, there were major battles.

During the fifties and sixties, the university undertook progressive planning; its leaders not only streamlined departments and colleges but also hired better faculty. The admission process was opened to diverse groups of students, including those from abroad. This trend was boosted by an exchange program between the university and the four eastern provinces of India. Under this contract, the agricultural scientists in these Indian states could earn their graduate degrees at the expense of their governments. Many professors at this university were also assigned to teach at universities in India. The scope of this contract did not cover me, as I was a private student educated in Canada and was admitted for a doctorate degree.

***

Having completed the coursework at the end of winter 1961, I was now assigned additional research projects. By the fall semester, I had given up my part-time job in the library and focused on my studies that mattered. Overall, I stayed on course.

Based on the evolving daily American life of a young foreign student, my post-Canada brain was appearing to be rewiring itself as it settled down to a new routine in this town. I became increasingly inquisitive about this much-admired modern Western society. Slowly but surely, what I liked most was the professed idea of American freedom and mobility. I thought it was wrong that most Indian students were keeping to themselves and mingling socially only among themselves. Socially, many felt intimidated, isolated, and imperfect to the American way of life. Because of racial and cultural barriers, the two had virtually nothing in common. The result was the creation of an Indian Cultural Association, under the auspices of which the younger students organized annual festivals such as Diwali, or festival of lights. All the Indian exchange students used this forum to invite their faculty advisers and landlords to an evening of fashion show, Indian food, and entertainment.

Unlike most foreign students, a handful of us coming from Canada or Europe (perhaps three or four naive young men) began to test our limits of social interactions. In addition to inviting our faculty advisers, we began to invite our classmates, both male and female, to Diwali festivals. Our Indian peers did not seem to object if these contacts were superficial.

That gave us an opportunity not only to celebrate our culture but also to invite non-Indians we had befriended. Mostly, it was aimed at reciprocating. Both Americans and non-Americans had been inviting us to their homes during Thanksgiving and Christmas. None of us had homes, so a university or church hall served that purpose. Invariably, a guest of honor was someone from the university community who had traveled to India or was an exchange scholar from there.

Once, an exchange faculty and his family from Chennai, India, were invited. They were the guests of honor at the 1960 Diwali celebrations. I met them there and was later invited to their home on a weekend. I met their son and daughter, who were looking for new friends in a strange town. They were disappointed they could not find anyone from their community. Their daughter, Neor Nish (NN), was a particularly sharp and modern girl. We got along well because we thought alike. I was, perhaps, the closest to her age.

Subsequently, she became a regular friend and attended many events with me. She confided that she had met a boy in Chennai and was attracted to him. She consistently talked about him in a way that somehow made me wonder about her choices in making friends. Did she not like her new friends? Her mother, contrary to her father, seemed overly concerned about her acquaintances with people like me or, for that matter, anyone else who she, the mother, did not choose.

One day, my friend, NN, confided in me about her mother's strange behaviors.

> From the age of ten my mother started comparing me with my brother. He was smarter and good-looking. As if that were not enough to feel snubbed, I began to doubt myself and felt abnormal and completely unflattering as a woman. By the age of fifteen, I noticed I had smaller boobs, and my nipples were big, dark, and round, as if my ancestors were from Africa.

I did not know how to respond. But it bothered me that an Indian mother would love her daughter less than she loved her son. Nevertheless, my reaction was in passing, and it did not endure.

One day, I ran into a group of students in the student union. Among them was a student from Canada. A few days later, I met her again. We had coffee together and chatted casually about our classes and what we planned to do in life. We met each other casually occasionally in the student common and, later, met quite regularly.

In our conversations, we shared our experiences in Canada and found something extremely coincidental. In our conversation one day, I dwelled on my encounter with a farmer during the summer while I was collecting field data in Ontario for my MA thesis. Seemingly a happenstance, that family had the same last name and was related to my new friend. That brought us closer and our relationship went far beyond just friends. I also became nostalgic for my days in Canada.

We could not be happy without seeing each other every day or at least every other day. This went on for close to half a year. Once she quoted her mother saying something about "us" that puzzled me. Her mother believed that some young Indians wanted to marry a Canadian to upgrade their social status.

My response was, "Look, here. I am concerned about how you would be accepted in my family, where, if a foreigner passes them by, they feel polluted and must take a bath."

She was alarmed at this portrayal. And we dropped the subject.

Even after hearing what I had to say about our mutual community unacceptance, she did not want to jeopardize our friendship, and we remained on good terms. Her mother was never mentioned to me again in any of our conversations. As we became affable and a bit open to each other, she began to focus on our bourgeoning relationship. I never thought of a long-term plan. Apparently, that did not preclude her from doing so. If she did, that would have been unilateral. I did not think anything would come out of that relationship.

As a modern youth, I was not an unusual foreign student from India, especially after I had steadied myself as a graduate student on campus. I was different in the sense that, unlike most others, I had lived in Canada before coming here. It was not uncommon for me, therefore, to be seen with members of the opposite sex, mostly in groups, in the student union.

Gradually, I noticed that some of the older Indian students, who were on an exchange program, began to whisper. One Bengali fellow, slightly younger-looking but not in his twenties as most of us were, began to show interest in conversing with me. He asked where I was from, and he introduced himself properly. He was not against socializing with the coeds as much as concerned about their range of friendships.

"Do you know how many boyfriends your girlfriend has?" he asked.

"Excuse me, is that what I think you just asked?"

"Yes. Do you know these girls are promiscuous?"

I objected, saying, "No, they are not."

Then he became defensive and apologetic and abruptly turned away, saying goodbye.

If nothing else, this bizarre conversation raised a central doubt in my mind. I began to wonder, what if?

No doubt I had given some thought to mature adult life as far as friendship, harmony, and like-mindedness was concerned but nothing beyond that. Sleeping with girlfriends while a student, no matter how tempting it was, was a bad idea, a very ruinous idea—not only because it could make our relationship awkward or worse, but also because I did not fully trust myself. I could get wrapped up in her and distracted from the one thing in life I did not want to be diverted from—my education, my career.

A normal social life is a human necessity. That is also natural. But could this Bengali fellow be too far ahead of me in judging people? Later, he made a few wacky remarks that are not worth writing about.

It turns out he had gotten married a few months before his arrival to this campus as a Bengal government employee to complete a master's degree. His marriage, his wife, and his new relationship were constantly on his mind. And he was looking for someone to share his perspectives. I decided he was not a belligerent man; he only had a bizarre outlook on life. Also, he had a uniquely old-fashioned, unpolished Indian way of conversing bluntly.

A week later, I happened to see him again. He apologized and assured me he had not wanted to be rude the other day. He invited me for coffee, and we went inside the student union and spent an hour talking. This time, he revealed to me that, in India, although marriages are arranged, the girls were invariably not virginal. They had had sex just for experience. He told me something that I, too, knew but did not realize how common it was. I knew three such cases. In the village where I worked, a young girl spent half a night with my teacher friend the night before her marriage ceremony. She lived right across from where my friend was renting a room. I attended her marriage, and while she was taking her marriage vows, I made eye contact with her. But she turned away, realizing I must have been privy to her rendezvous.

Mukherjee revealed to me that he and his wife had intercourse before marriage just to make sure they were compatible. "Why not with me, instead of some other fellow?" he said. "Moral codes have nothing to do with sex prohibition," he lectured. "Romantic attraction and infatuation are all about bonding and making connection," he persisted.

A week later, some of us, including a married Indian couple and my coed companion, had organized a picnic at a creek not far from the campus. We piled in two cars and carried food and drink. We decided to take along with us Mukherjee, who we felt was lonely and missed his wife. Others in my group knew a bit about him through me and were curious to know his views on family matters. As a pseudo philosopher, he was familiar with the original version of *Kama Sutra* by Vatsayana. He knew when to speak in generalities and when to share his personal experiences. He stated, "It is good to know the meaning of love, romance, and sex. These are, in essence, inherently joined together, and they govern our lives."

We were awed by his definitive statements.

"A relationship should be an activity between just the two people involved. When people are brought from outside into this equation, as it is in India or wherever they practice arranged marriages, it can create some of the most unsolvable stumbling blocks," he concluded.

According to the philosopher Kautilya, the Gāndharva forms of marriage based upon mutual love between the parties to matrimony required the approval of both the parents. He divulged, "It is a sin according to Kautilya to allow a girl's periods to go in vain after she is engaged to marry. A man can have sexual intercourse with his intended woman who has not been received by him for cohabitation for the period of her seven menstruations."

All these statements, authoritatively spoken, were too bold for us to relate to and finally the Indian woman spoke up and argued that the arranged marriages of India were more permanent. Those who bring two people together know things based on their experience and observations. She advised, "Relationships that are based on just one of the ingredients alone are unsustainable."

Mukherjee agreed with her remarks, but he was trying to put the burden of building relationships on just two people. He believed that two people in love had to form a relationship on mutual attraction. "There is a polarity involved here, like light and dark, masculine, and feminine. It is awesomely powerful, and it is in everything. It is that electricity that draws the two lovers together," he concluded.

The married Indian woman in our group vehemently objected to the suggestion that Mukherjee was professing sex before marriage.

Mukherjee replied, "I am sorry, but having sex before marriage is the best choice for nearly everyone. How do I know? Well, first, most everyone has sex before marriage—95 percent of Americans do not wait until their wedding night. And that is a longstanding American value. Even among folks in my grandparents' generation, nine out of ten of them had sex before they wed, not necessarily with their future wives. That was the difference."

We were stunned to hear the above assertion and, in unison, shook our heads in disagreement. My friend, who I did not think went to church and was listening quietly to the above dialogue, suddenly burst out and referred to the Bible, where supposedly Jesus said, "So, they are no longer two, but one" (Matthew 19:6 NIV).

Echoed Mukherjee, "But one, one flesh! What is that? Doesn't that refer to sexual intercourse? This physical bonding brings great joy when nurtured and secured by love and commitment. But it brings great pain if it is broken. So, to bless and protect us, God commands that this profound closeness should occur only between people who are going to be committed to each other in marriage."

This profound statement, backed by a holy book, seemed to conclude the discussion, and we all felt it to be an ultimate remark. We also looked at the darkening sky and decided it was time to wrap up the picnic and return to the campus and prepare for morning classes.

Life was quite hectic for a graduate student. And at times, it felt miserable doing the same things—studying, attending classes, writing term papers, preparing for exams, working on assigned projects, studying in the library for hours, ad infinitum. There was no pastime, no source of entertainment, and no pleasure. At times, we suffered utter boredom. It was only on weekends that we met our friends in the student commons. On some evenings, we would either meet someone new, or an old friend would share an entertaining gossip or a fairy tale!

One social activity for me consisted of joining a group of mixed acquaintances who gathered on most weekends in the student union after dinner, a sort of kaffeeklatsch. More frequent visitors to this group were a solitary economics professor, several foreign students, and a few curious local students, both male and female. Sometimes, our Indian exchange students would also stop by to see what was going on. We would normally discuss global issues collectively. Individually, however, we would seek out one or two who would share accomplishments and offer solutions to our problems.

One of the highlights of the year, especially for those of Indian background, was the annual Diwali dinner and entertainment, mentioned earlier. We would invite our academic adviser and his wife to this event. They would have been the only ones who would have entertained us at their home on Christmas Day. We would all dress up in our native costumes and have a smashing time. It was for this event that I invited my Canadian friend from our group to be my guest at the annual function. Usually, my guest would have been the newly arrived guest from India, Ms. NN, but because of her unique situation, she could not be available.

Mixing by gender and race at social gatherings on a university campus was considered platonic and harmless—unless the racial barrier was crossed. To that extent, we were safe and indomitable because we were, at best, not treated as unimportant by the dominant class. Therefore, the most correct way of liking other human beings was to express one's mind in terms of love of divinity. In short, with genuine platonic love, the stunning companion tended to inspire the mind and the soul and directed one's attention to spiritual things. Socrates, in Plato's *Symposium*, explained two types of love—earthly love and godly love. Earthly love is nothing but mere material attraction for physical pleasure and reproduction. Godly love begins the drive from physical attraction but transcends gradually to love for supreme beauty. This concept of divine love was later transformed into the term *platonic love*.

***

My confidante from Canada graduated and went home for the summer. As to our relationship, though more alarming in the eyes of the older Indian exchange students, it remained cursory from my perspective. These government civil servants were concerned about my future as a foreign student. One referred to me as a non-Indian. I found these people strange. They came in four groups from four different Indian states and kept to themselves. Their social life was confined, and they kept their distance from the local people.

Quite the contrary, the younger Indian and other Asian students were outgoing and mingled freely with the local population. After all, they had come to a different country, a unique society, to experience openness and freedom. They had come to be educated and to experience what life had to offer. They were confident in themselves and tolerant of diversity, unlike the older Indian civil servants who came on a foreign jaunt—an all-expenses-paid retreat. They were spending their jolly time here on a paid pretend vacation.

Some of us went further and got to know people we befriended on a personal level. We were young, and the same thing would have happened even if we had stayed in our own countries. So, what if we got to know chosen members of the opposite sex? As for romance, our relationships were founded on deliberate limits and carefully, rationally considered bounds. Mine seemed to be ending along coolly considered lines. My Canadian friend seemed erratic and premature in bringing her mother to meet me without consulting me. And when she did arrive, I was already in another bourgeoning relationship, which I did not want to jeopardize.

From the beginning what I had been most concerned about my Canadian friend was her sense of contradictory views on Indians. At one point, she thought she was being used as a tool to advance my interests, and at another, she was planning to get married. I told her there were too many family and societal hurdles we must consider seriously. At least my mother had to be informed.

She went to the bathroom and came out bare breasted and implored, "Please make love to me!"

I was shocked and said, "No. I can't make love to you." To lighten up the air, I asked, "How did you get the merkin to adhere?"

"Nonsense," she shouted. "That is just me. I have hair. I am human, unlike some foreign students, who take a cue from their mothers in matters of romance."

Her mood changed. And after getting dressed, she became scalding mad. She screamed and slammed the door behind her. That was the end of an innocuous but impulsive friendship.

Luckily, that was the last time I saw her. No doubt it was a scary experience. I was literally frightfully distressed. I was not seeking emotional involvement. I guess she hoped for the best in her favor in the long run, when I would fall in love with her. I always wondered if she found someone to marry and settle down with after a raucous life while a foreign student in the United States. All she wanted was someone to stroke her ego and calm her down!

Following that, for at least a week, I had a series of dreams centering on the topic. She would be sitting in the car's passenger seat, taking off her blouse and undoing her bra. Then she would offer her left breast to the stranger sitting in the driver's seat. He would literally devour it. Horrified, I would wake up and find myself sweating. I could not figure out what that was all about. But once I'd realized how asinine the dream was, it must have waned from my memory.

It was around this time a dear old friend, Ms. NN, was back in town, moving into a dormitory and getting ready to resume her studies. She called me several times. But knowing what she must have gone through, I was unwilling to hear her sad story. It would be unpleasant to say the least.

One evening, after I had returned from the library at ten o'clock and had just changed into my pajamas and was sitting on my bed absorbed in a deep thought, I heard a mild knock on the door. "Who is it?"

"It's me," someone whispered. "Can I come in please?"

I opened the door, and it was someone I least expected. "Come in, come in, and take a seat." I pointed to my chair.

I went back to sitting where I was and asked, "So, how are things going?"

"Not very well," she replied sadly. "You know my mother has never loved me, and that is why this has happened to me. In childish rebellion, I dated this guy who promised to marry me. But suddenly, he has disappeared. I miss him and hate myself." Her sobbing became more pronounced. "Can you please hold me? I am hurting, and I have no one to share my agony."

I motioned for her to come and sit next to me. She embraced me and started crying, tears pouring down my left shoulder. I could feel the wetness. That was a clumsy position to be sitting side by side, so I scooted back against the wall. That is when she put her head on my lap and continued to sob. Pretty soon, we were lying side by side and kissing and touching each other. I held her breast and noted that they were not small.

"Not now. And be careful. They are still oozing," she whispered.

By now, both of us were aroused and there was no way stopping the inevitable. I kissed her boobies; she warned I might have to swallow the milk since it had been just a short time ago that she had given birth to her baby. Then she spread her legs and held my hard penis. Moving closer, she inserted me deep inside her. I felt her hot breath on my face. She was still very emotional. "I have been hurt so badly, but this feels right." With me buried deep inside her, she went on sobbing and tightly holding onto me. Then she whispered, "Start moving and do it deliberately and slowly."

I did what I was told.

She was now relaxed, jubilant, lifted, and truly ready to lead a typical life.

As we held each other, I reminded her that we were still young and would likely meet a lot of people, and someday the right partner would turn up. That seemed to make sense to both of us. "So," I suggested, "let's make some sweet tea and have it with the leftover apple pie."

***

Before the above twist of fate, some two months earlier, my former Canadian friend had inquired if I would deliver a couple of plants and a few other items to her friend who lived in a building some walking distance from my own. Hence, at my convenience, I delivered the items to a rather innocent-looking, graceful woman, who was thankful for my gesture. I must have been in a hurry, and she was unable to thank me profusely. But she must have known about me, as later that week, she called to thank me and wondered if I visited the student union sometimes. I told her when I could be there. On weekends, as was noted earlier, I went there on a regular basis, usually to meet friends.

The next time I went, there she was with Ms. Pat Smith, a known member of the group.

Considering shaky past friendships, the ancestral spirits were prompting me to follow my instincts, and grace would follow. *That is your destiny.* Until now, my student life was an open book, and I was amenable to new friendships. But I was very guarded. Yet, when our eyes met, I became inquisitive. Along with Pat, the three of us walked over to the coffee shop, and we conversed about our studies and mutual friends. She, too, was a nursing student.

***

In Europe, during the Middle Ages, marriages were sanctified by the church. Hence, the troubadour notion of a real person-to-person *amor* was extremely dangerous. Not only that, it was also heresy; it was spiritual adultery punishable by death. Therefore, all marriages were arranged by society and sanctified by church. Surely, we now live in tranquil times, certainly not in Europe's past.

For me, it was a joyfully critical time. I was moving toward a life-altering phase filled with love, and a natural pull was in control. My new friend and I met several times, and we became aware of our mutual interests.

She invited me to a college town where she had graduated from before transferring to this campus. There, she had a host family who had shepherded her during her student days. I was taken there, apparently, so they could ascertain what kind of a person I was and what I stood for. There, I was treated very well and welcomed into their circle of friends. We became closer, developing an affectionate care I had never experienced before. It felt genuine. There was a mutual respect for each other's culture and religion. I did not sense any feeling of distance or differences that separated people of the West and the East. There was honesty.

I was young, inexperienced, and possibly naive. Little did I know that, to snare a husband, girls in this culture are trained to listen a lot, nod a lot, widen their eyes, and be thrilled with everything the boy of their choice said. But it seemed odd that her parents were not involved at that point.

***

When the exam week was over, I went to see my new friend in her apartment. And as we were finishing our small talk, I wanted to make sure she was aware there were numerous social, cultural, racial, and religious differences between us. She assured me she was quite aware of that. But I was not sure.

Therefore, I stated, "If you are really prone to adapting and willing to live a life of unity out of diversity, why not change your religion to Hinduism?"

One could see a ghost in her face, and tears began to stream down her cheeks. As I reached out and embraced her, she wrapped her arms around my back. I held the side of her head, and she nestled it into my chest. I sensed a closeness to her, and she felt protected. We were silent for a great while, perhaps evaluating the meaning of all this honesty and closeness. As we parted that evening, we were in accord that each would respect the other's religion.

I was raised as a Hindu in North India. My new friend was a Christian from the Midwest of the United States. Normally, it would be an incongruous relationship. Before marriage through occasional dialogues, we tacitly agreed that our religious upbringing was unique to us, and we would honor that fact. Presumably, it would not take us long into our marriage to realize we shared the same values and worldview, even though we expressed those sentiments in a different spiritual language. That was what religion was, a language made up of symbols and metaphors that allowed people to communicate to themselves and to others the indescribable experience of faith and grace.

I already spoke her spiritual language—in other words, the idioms of Christianity. And she learned about mine as she mingled with other Indian couples on campus and, notably, enrolled in India's art and culture classes on campus. And then we became spiritually bilingual. A religion was only as good as the people who adhered to its teachings. The outcome was that we were in a genuinely serious relationship.

Compared to then, now there are so many atypical options that young college students get exactly what they want without commitment. It is akin to a buffet; sometimes even before they realize what they seek, they have secured it. It is a sign of how far this society has come that relationship labels are no longer two-sizes-fit-all. Marriage is not a fixed choice anymore.

No doubt, we were, at least in those days, on a common track, and our companionship flourished. I invited my faculty adviser to the 1961 Diwali dinner, organized by the campus India Association, and there, I introduced him to my intended. By that time, we were nearly engaged. The professor was not enthusiastic about the bourgeoning alliance. Be that as it may, slowly, I began to meet friends and relatives of my intended. The road was being paved for an effortless courtship.

Courtship is the period in a couple's relationship that precedes their engagement and marriage or the establishment of an agreed-upon relationship of a more enduring kind. During courtship, a couple gets to know each other and decides if there will be a continuing platonic friendship, a wait-and-see situation, a temporary live-in arrangement, a short engagement, a long one, or none at all. Traditionally, in the case of a formal engagement, it has been perceived that it is the role of a male to actively "court" or "woo" a female, thus encouraging her to understand him and be receptive to a proposal of marriage. In many Western societies, these distinct gender roles have lost some of their importance. It is now common for females of younger generations both to initiate relationships and to propose marriage.

In more closed societies, courtship is virtually eliminated altogether by the practice of an arranged marriage, as in India, where partners are chosen for young people, typically by their parents. All trial and serial courtship is forbidden. Sanctioning only arranged matches implies guarding outwardly the chastity of young people. And partly, it is a matter of furthering family interests, which in such cultures may be considered more important than individual romantic appeals.

Over recent decades, though, the concept of arranged marriages has changed or simply been mixed with other forms of dating. This is the case with newer Asian Indian traditions, in which potential couples could meet and date each other before they decide to continue their relationship.

***

Having completed all my coursework, I took a comprehensive written PhD examination and waited for an oral examination sometime soon. At the end of the second year, along with finishing my coursework, I also completed a foreign language (German) requirement. Plus, I had published two technical articles, "The Mathematical Formulation of Production Functions" and "Statistical Measurement of Variances for MPP and MRS."

Should not entering upon matrimonial empyrean be an accomplishment? Indeed, the highest part of heaven, believed to have existed in ancient Greek and Roman times, contained a pure form of love. Even some Christians thought it to be the dwelling place of God, who blesses those in love. That is a grace equal to the highest triumph. So, it could also be integrated in a graduate student's progress report. Would that not please one's intended, if not the faculty adviser?

One day, I ran into a professor who had taught a methodology class that I had completed. I told him that, based on the term paper I'd submitted for his class, I had published two articles in a major research journal. He said, "I will change your grade to an A—that is, if you haven't earned it already."

I was appalled and began to wonder about the professor's judgment criteria in grading the research papers of foreign students.

Be that as it may, as scheduled by my adviser, an oral examination was held before a committee consisting of four members, one being from an external department. There was one junior faculty member who did not participate, just listened. The questions were simple, essentially theoretical, and I was able to answer all of them.

As per my Canadian training, at the end of answering each of the questions raised, I added my own assessment of the theoretical framework. For instance, the production function has its application in evaluating the stages an enterprise can go through before it peaks. At the end of an hour and a half of questions and answers, I was asked to wait in the adjacent room while the committee deliberated. Though a bit anxious, I was confident that the outcome would be positive. I was called in. But the only one in the room was my adviser. He told me the committee would like to talk to me again during the next semester. That was after my impending matrimony. He assured me everything would be all right—that this was just a routine matter.

At this stage of my abiding in the American cultural milieu, I was, no doubt, allured by the freedom of nonrational thought, for that is where soft subjects such as intuition, faith, and love are founded. I was in love—pure and simple. No distraction, threat, or promises could lure me away. I was ready to face it all. Decisions concerning my future could be liberating, or they could signify a point of no return. My fiancée and I had now bonded and were on the same wavelength.

My decision to marry her was about to rock the known and unknown segments of my life. Exceedingly shattering letters were received from my brothers, my mother, and a sister-in-law. It did create a ripple effect, in that I did not realize how intensely they wanted me to return from the United States, socially unscathed! Perhaps they knew something I did not. Or was it simply about their way?

As planned, my marriage was scheduled in a town adjacent to Kansas City. It went as expected—a time for celebration and family joy. But my kinfolk could not be there due to distance. Instead, I had a token representative from my side—Dr. Nathan Chaco, a visiting scholar and his wife, Sonya, from South India, along with my supportive Indian foreign students from campus. My fiancée, on the other hand, had a large family who came to the wedding and rejoiced in the event.

We were staying at a friend's house. Also with us was Grandma Hughes from Colorado. On the day of the wedding when everyone went to the chapel in preparation for the afternoon ceremonies, Grandma stayed back, keeping an eye on me, lest I might back down or abscond.

When Grandma and I arrived at the chapel, I was moved by the number of people who were already seated in the chapel. There was a contingency of younger Indian students from the university, along with my two best friends—Surjit and Ron. Also in attendance was my graduate adviser, Dr. Rufus Kleinmann; though not enthusiastic about this union, he felt he had to attend. I was saddened that my own mother and brothers could not be there. But that was understandable. A local pastor performed the ceremony and administered the oath of marriage. To restrain my emotions was critical. Each word was being taped.

After the ceremony, everyone was invited to a grand reception at our host's residence. They were the most gracious people I had ever known. The evening stretched on and on. People expected us to leave on our honeymoon, but we were enjoying the limelight. Eventually, we left and went to our hotel room, totally exhausted.

The following day, we began our journey back to our apartment. On our way back, I began to feel depressed. On the one hand, I was happy. But the unfinished task with respect to my degree work was casting a dark shadow. The thought of the improbable "what-if" began to give me chills. No doubt I was wrestling with the mysterious dark clouds lurking on the horizon. What had to transpire was destiny. I was the author of that, if not solely.

Commonly, each impulsive move has its own gloomy outcome. Two weeks after our arrival back in town, I went to my graduate office and found the atmosphere cold and even bitter; no one would talk to me. When everyone in our graduate student office left, an older student who was working on his MA degree came over and warned me that I had taken a step that might prove to be problematic for me. He did not mention the word *marriage*, but his comment was directed at that. He came face-to-face with me and shared the rumor that everyone was whispering—that my recent marriage to an American White girl was a shotgun marriage. Amused, he reiterated, "Well, that's the gossip." I did not understand what the phrase meant at the time.

Later in the day, I received a phone call from my adviser about my oral examination that was scheduled for the following Monday. I felt good about my prospect for overcoming this hurdle too. I began to focus on my specialization. But there was no indication of what kind of questions would be asked or that the answers would be acceptable to the members of the committee.

The committee consisted of my iniquitous adviser, another junior faculty from the same department, and two professors from outside the department. A senior member from the other department was a much older professor with a cutting demeanor. He asked most of the questions, and we got entangled about why some areas of the world are rich and others poor. Why do some countries prosper, and others remain poor and oppressed?

At the peak of this discourse on poverty versus prosperity, my focus was on Adam Smith, who wrote his famous book, *Wealth of Nations*, in 1776. Early economists were essentially fixated with the explanation supporting the causation on solely cultural terms. They argued that a country's penchants, beliefs, and values determined the nature and extent of its economic growth. Smith argued that, for market economies to thrive, a peculiar norm is required that would promote self-interest. But certain other societies that believed in fate, as in Asia, hedged on being acquisitive to the point it brought failure to their potential rise of capitalism—also referred to as oriental despotism. So far, it was a soft argument to stand on. But when Max Weber came out with his definitive thesis focusing on work ethics in his 1905 book, *Protestant Ethic and the Spirit of Capitalism*, religion of the West was centered as the primary reason Western countries had prospered and others had not.

The senior member on my committee, being a staunch Christian of the Calvinistic variety, wanted me to accept the thesis that non-Western countries would never advance economically unless they adopt the Weberian formula. Respectfully, I submitted that, coming from a former British colony that was dirt poor, I had a compartmentalized cultural spectrum that encompasses Hinduism in devotional matters and acquisitiveness as my karmic dharma. The latter crafted me as a rational and a pragmatic person. "I am action-oriented, and that is why

I am a student here in a thoroughly Western society where you are my teacher."

He said, "That combination will not work, and you should change your approach."

That is where the Q and A session ended.

In retrospect, during the mid-twentieth century, all these cultural justifications for economic growth began to crumble when Japan's economy took off, along with those of the East Asian countries known as the "four tigers." They sure smashed the Weberian concept that Western culture alone could attain economic growth. China enlarged the scope of the four tigers by spreading its export-oriented economic paradigm and overwhelming the Western domination.

In fact, I do not remember anyone else asking questions. After an hour or so, my adviser escorted me back to the building, where our offices were located and gave me the bad news. "You did not satisfy the committee."

I asked, "Why?"

No specific reasons were given.

The following day, I was told that my candidacy for the PhD degree had been terminated, and if I so preferred, the department would consider granting me a master's degree based on just the coursework.

I replied in an irritated tone, "I already have a master's degree from a prestigious Canadian university." I made it clear I was offended by the suggestion.

And their response was a final strike. I was asked to vacate the office I was occupying in the graduate student area and return the key. It was akin to being thrown into a cesspit.

This episode had multiple effects; a chain reaction was on the horizon in that I was not a student anymore and would not receive any financial assistance as a graduate research assistant. I would have no justification to stay at this university and the US Immigration Office would soon deport me. I had never in a million years anticipated such a calamity. Everything I had done in my life so far had been nullified.

A committee had sentenced me to a psychological death! I wondered if my Canadian professors would have led me on so far and suddenly, cruelly, knocked me down. I was a naive young man whose fault was not related to academic achievement but, rather, that I had crossed the unspoken racial barrier.

I began to explore the alternatives of finding a university that would accept me as a graduate student in my field. I wrote to many universities and to two professors I had met at conferences. They advised me that no university in the United States would accept me as a graduate student, knowing that a department on another campus had terminated my candidacy for the doctorate.

It took me a while to feel the full impact of that devastating decision by an injudicious department committee. It was like falling into a deep hole. "Now what the hell am I supposed to do, just roll over and die?" I kept yelling.

I was not into drinking alcohol to drown my sorrows. Who should I fight with and for what reason? Whither my self-respect? I mean, there was nothing to do but blame myself for coming to America. I should have stayed in Canada or accepted that job in Guyana or returned to India after completing my master's degree in Canada. I had been ahead then. At times, I was simply furious. I was fighting with myself. It was a kind of an allegory for what had happened to so many African Americans, Native Indians, and minorities, who were punished by American society for being who they were in essence, irrespective of their accomplishments.

It is not easy for members of minority groups in America to maintain a normal life, much less seek superiority. For most of its history, America did pretty much everything a country could do to impose a narrative of inferiority on its non-White population. Over and over, African Americans have fought back against this plot, but its legacy endures even today. Case in point is President Barrack Obama, who was elected to the US presidency twice. But the White power elite, especially in the Congress of the United States, could not tolerate his presence in the

White House. Even when Asians are not on the firing line, they certainly face the collateral damage. Now they are even a direct target.

The foundation of fear of equality, precipitated by the presence of the non-Whites, persists in every institution of America. Nothing is spared, not even families, churches, and institutions of learning. It is a built-in mechanism in America's social milieu. President Lyndon Johnson correctly stated, "America has the crippling legacy of bigotry and injustice, because to be Black or Brown in White society is not to stand on equal ground."

There is an ever-present tendency to pull down those outsiders who are threatening to break down the barriers. The same institutional factors that caused poverty—bigotry, denial of education, lack of job opportunities, and discrimination in voting—are sapping away our self-assurance that might give us success in life. Once belittling is entrenched, poverty becomes the norm.

Under these circumstances, it took me a great deal of energy and determination to muster more grit, more drive, and the exceptional amount of hard work it would take to crawl out of the cesspool. I could not have done it myself but for a few angels, even on this dusky campus. Along with them, it was the invisible hand of our creator that was the real force behind my fortuitous recovery.

In the United States, people talk of equality of opportunity. But this equity applies only to the dominant class or to White immigrants. For the minority, the idea is simply transformed into equality of outcome and what that possibility signifies. Once you become a competitor, you are a clear threat and a challenge to the White prerogative for preferred jobs. White privileged classes in American society are, indeed, fearful of equality. They shudder if they must compete with people of color. For the latter, even equality of opportunity is just a misplaced cliché. Excluded from equal treatment were not just Black and Brown men but also women.

A century and a half ago, like Black and foreign students, women too were not admitted to this university. One wonders if, indeed, they were a threat to the university. Or was it the other way around? After having been assessed, finally the coeds gained full admission to the university some ninety years later. Selected foreign students were also brought into the student body after that. The earlier groups were older, docile, settled in life, and were not only representing their governments but were also financed by them.

As pioneers, when women were first brought to this campus some century and a half ago, they were protected from the lecherous menfolk of the university. Some openly feared that men would molest them. That is why they were not only segregated but were also housed on the periphery of the campus, which "lacked beauty and convenience."

It was a bold and hazardous decision to allow women to get some training in the art of teaching in public schools. But they were barred from lecture halls, the chapel, and even the library. Later, when no incidents were reported, they were marched in groups as if they were inmates, with teachers in the front and the back, to recitations and lectures on the main campus. By degrees, when they proved to be of no threat to the morals, they were admitted to all the classes and in every academic department. Thereupon, they excelled over their classmates of the opposite gender and disproportionately achieved academic kudos.

The saga of the admission of Black students was much involved, circuitous, and tragic. But when young foreign students like myself arrived from the backyards of Canada, Australia, and Europe, it too was a bold step on the part of the university. We were under scrutiny so no harm would come to us. Few uniquely cultural utterances were alien to us, such as when older White men would call to us, "Hey, boy!"

We were also confused when we would find ourselves walking alone, and the White student groups would jeer at us and say, "You don't belong here." We had been admitted by the same university they were!

The university had a network of proxies who kept track of us. Often, they came between us and the danger. Among ourselves, we shared this observation, especially when we came to know that our academic advisers knew of our whereabouts. They knew who we met, which shops we frequented, and when we went to the movie halls.

This university was one of the last land-grant colleges to allow African Americans as students. Indeed, it was the Supreme Court ruling that integrated the campus. I could only imagine the agony of those people, who had weathered the outcome of their own fate one way or the other. I wished to have cried on their shoulders. I would have asked them to lend a hand or just listen to my painful tale.

John Updike once wrote, "America is a vast conspiracy to make you happy." Indeed, it taught me to hate America and to love it at the same time. Well, all my happiness was gone. It was sudden, abrupt, and unexpected. Also, all my freedom and accomplishments had been taken away from me. There was no joy; all that was left was despair and despondency.

Yet the human mind has a lot of built-in mechanisms for coping with such utter disappointments—that is, if the victims do not kill themselves. After a while, you just tell yourself to get up from the gutter, shake the dirt off, and wash your face and mind. That is where hope comes from—from just standing up.

The hidden voice of the angels echoed in my ears: *Do not blame yourself. Now you belong here. Turn to those who would help the underdogs. There are angels out there waiting for you. Take part in life again. Don't you dare drop out!*

Hence, hope came alive. It was probably there all along—since hope dies last (*la esperanza muere ultima*).

Without hope, there would not emerge a determination to go on with life. So long as there was hope, I felt determined in my actions. With the Almighty's grace, I became active and alive again. I felt empowered. It happened only when I overcame the feeling that *it was my fault*! I became a different person, radiating with humility; and then others looked at me differently. I did not just disappear. I was back. Yes, I belong here.

One day an Anglo student who knew me spoke to me sympathetically outside the library and said, "What they did to you was unjust and unfair."

I replied, "I forgave them. I am fine now."

Soon thereafter, I met a junior member of my past stained committee in the student union who greeted me and asked if I could have coffee with him. At first, I hesitated, but I agreed. He too was very apologetic and made it apparent to me that he was on the committee only as a nontenured junior faculty. Obviously, the senior faculty members, he hinted, had made up their minds beforehand. He wished me well, and I never saw him again.

Seemingly, such decisions are made at higher levels of hierarchy. Grown-up and intelligent people are also capable of unfairness, and they exhibit callous disregard for budding scholars who do not pass their litmus test. It is the devil who controls their actions.

Later, I came to know that a colonel in the US Army had also complained to the university president that a foreign student was befriending his daughter. "That must be put to an end," he had warned. No red-blooded American parent wanted his daughter to marry a foreigner and to lose his or her progeny to a foreign land.

In an ostensibly liberated environment of a university campus, such friendships were developing endlessly. But no sociological studies were undertaken. Only recently did we read about the fate of President Barack Obama's father, who was working on his PhD degree at Harvard University. But when Harvard's WASPy authorities got wind of Obama senior's White women friends, they revoked his scholarship and forced him to return to Kenya before he could complete his dissertation.

For me, seeing the hoary, devilish folks on campus brought back the old painful memories. The past bad news rekindled a disappointment of the nth degree, which was pulverizing my whole being daily and in a progressive manner. At times in my wounded moments, I would be sad and depressed. In those moments, I would question my worth again. Was life worth living now that I had lost out? A patient with hope, a health provider will agree, has a better chance of recovery than I had at that point.

I was still filled with despair. With prospects devastated, a sense of paranoia related to survival often sets in; hope was replaced by concerns that eroded my confidence, which in turn fostered more fear, and—well, we get the picture. I was continuously in a state of shocked disbelief. What else could go wrong? Why would it not?

Worries over survival in this perceived hostile environment were eating me up. I was losing sleep, bawling continuously, and binging on toast and tea for comfort. On the urging of my dejected wife, I reluctantly began to see a psychiatrist for help. This counselor got me involved with tutoring one of her younger patients, who needed help with social studies. That exercise was designed to restore my confidence.

What would it take to reinstate my faith in my ability as a student and a scholar? Likely, it would take two things—first, clear thinking and, second, self-determination. Clear thinking required total focus on new possibilities and negating the old altogether. It would be almost impossible to read about a story of a foreign student getting dragged to hell in the way I had been and then coming back publicly and assuredly, boasting about the purported reason for recovery. It would have to be via an unforeseen force of a spiritual nature.

Recalling my inner dialogue on the bus ride from Canada to the United States calmed me down. I had to walk away from the past. Ostensibly, the developing hatred toward the evil committee was a toxin that was feeding my fears. *I must escape that trap. How do I do that?*

Self-regulation has to do with self-reliance, self-confidence, and mindfulness. Until now, I had not reacted to how people behaved around me and what they knew about me. What did they expect of me?

Seemingly, fellow sycophant graduate students, out of sheer jealousy mixed with racism, concocted spurious stories about my social life and slipped those to my gullible professors. Many of those students, out of envy, were spiteful, and their true intentions became questionable. I learned a lesson the hard way. I should have singularly focused on my studies and not accepted camaraderie and, thus, subjected myself to treachery from the native graduate students. They were like snakes ready to strike and inject their venom in unsuspecting, naive foreign students who were far ahead of them in intellect and culture.

I was soon coming to a dead end, when providence prompted me to seek out professors in the College of Arts and Sciences (CAS) who served as advisers for foreign students. One day, as I was entering the CAS office building, I met a foreign student who was coming out of the building. He stopped to talk to me, and after learning a bit about my predicament, he urged me to go in and talk to his adviser. Later, I learned that the student I had just met was from Jordan, was married to an American woman, and had transferred to the College of Arts and Sciences from the College of Agriculture. He graduated with his PhD and, soon after I had met him, went back to his country.

Noted Vedic sages of the Indian subcontinent had taught their disciples that the danger that threatened their existence contained within its fold a means to escape it. Where there was peril, there was a relief; right there emerged a saving skill. That is the genius of human psyche. One must seek a way to escape destruction. I realized that is where I, too, had to find an answer to allay the risk of my destruction. Hence, I must look for an open door.

Good fortune and grace invariably go together. When society punishes outsiders for having dared to reach to the level of the dominant class, for doing anything that would also excite envy, conditions are created to mete out punishment in the form of mental deprivation and an end to that individual's prospects. I had been punished for aiming for equality—a punishment that had resulted in my total poverty of mind and body. I truly felt I belonged to this society because I was being fully initiated and browbeaten. My deprivation and failure were society's problem as well. This is how I understood and accepted the concept and practice of justice. With divine assistance, I was fortunate to have understood this lesson and found peace. After all, the self-governing dogma of this society emphasizes only free speech, religious liberty, and jury trials. It does not include equality. Indeed, there is a general "fear of equality" in America.

The advice given to me by a junior professor in the College of Arts and Sciences on campus was to "start taking classes" as soon as possible. "You need to prove yourself as a potential student in our discipline," he said, making his point clear. I could feel a door opening for me. It was now up to me to prove myself and salvage my life.

Having discussed the details of my future plans with my soulmate, I decided to enroll in the required classes in a new field during the summer of 1962. The courses I was enrolled in were American Political Thought, Problems of International Politics, and Research Methodology. I enjoyed those topics; the professors were erudite and exceedingly knowledgeable. They were also fair-minded. I absorbed their teachings and made excellent grades. That was awfully encouraging. At last, there was some solace, and I saw light at the far end of the tunnel. But I was still angst-ridden; what if the former faculty of the rogue department objected to my starting over in another department on the same university campus? Basically, it was a risky move. But I was a risk-taker anyway, having left a secure homeland, a promising career, and job prospects while in Canada.

Be that as it may, I continued taking the prescribed courses with the consent of my new and angelic advisers and fulfilled all the requirements. As a continuing student, I received a Curator's Grant-in-Aid for tuition deferment for the remainder of my graduate studies. My faculty adviser and other professors gave me unreserved, compassionate support. They were my guardian angels. Since I had taken all the required courses, I was advised I should now opt for an MA degree promptly as a steppingstone to a PhD. I thought that was an expedient move. Then no one could make an objection to my status as a prior student in another department on the same campus. This was my second master's degree in North America.

Many Midwestern universities have come a long way. Whereas a century and a half ago, they filled vacancies based entirely on religious affiliations and political persuasions, the enlightened leaders searched far and wide for meritorious faculty and staff, with a bent toward reorganization and knowledge expansion. That progressive mindedness among top leaders was what made these institutions achieve excellence and primed them for future challenges.

But the changes were not even. And some of the old prejudices—born out of the classically bound institutions of learning of the nineteenth century—persisted in tiny provincial pockets. For example, when my wife went to register and pay for her spring semester courses, she was asked to pay a higher tuition fee that applied to foreign students. "Why do I have to pay a higher tuition?" she objected.

"Because you are married to a foreign student," she was told.

My wife strongly protested. The registrar then consulted the old statutes that had expired. She accepted their apologies and continued attending her classes.

***

That summer of 1964, I was honored to have been selected as a fellow to attend the Inter-University Consortium for Research at another Midwest land-grant campus up north. I was the only student from my university. The students at the consortium were from major institutions in the United States of America, Canada, Europe, and Asia. The professors were the best in their fields. The four courses I enrolled in that summer earned me straight A's. The courses were taught by guest scholars from the New England area and the upper Midwest.

Indeed, reincarnation occurs in many forms. It can be of body, mind, or status. I was reembodied, indeed salvaged, after a dead end from one academic discipline to another that proved to be extremely amicable, gratifying, and enriching. When we are bumped off and then survive and are brought back in another walk of life, we need not lament, grieve, or look back. We should neither blame anyone nor go back to our annihilator for revenge.

For an adjusted person, who I became, undertaking retribution was out of the question. I was powerless. Vengeance is not what helps the victim anyway. When someone has power over you, there is no winnable recourse. Instead, the attitude should be of love—love thine enemy. In this way, the oppressor is flattered into oblivion, and you win the game by escaping his final blow.

In retrospect, my wife and I were not only amazed but also wondered how and why I could have come out of the dead end if it had not been for the intercession of a higher power. Indeed, in our trials and tribulations, the Holy Spirit not only helps us endure but also toughens us. Not only did it show me the way, but it also mellowed the opponents.

Having received my MA, I was automatically a genuine scholar of my discipline. The result was that it confirmed my candidacy for the doctorate program. My adviser had talked to a foreign language professor who was eager to certify that I had, earlier, passed the required foreign language examination and that the result remained valid.

During the two-year period I was taking courses in the fine arts discipline, I made a point of not mingling with fellow graduate students outside the classroom. But there was one person who was eager to talk to me. And I, too, felt comfortable chatting with him whenever we happened to meet in the student union lounge. He had been taking courses for a while, whenever he could secure a leave of absence from his teaching job. He and I used to reminisce about being a student in perpetuity. Providence had it that this senior fellow student, an African American who was on an extended leave of absence to finish his dissertation, asked me one day if I was interested in accepting a teaching job in New Orleans. Later, I realized who might have been behind that prodding—his adviser was Dr. Robert B. Kenberry, one of my valued mentors.

There was a core of seen and unseen angelic professors on this otherwise maligned campus who wanted me to succeed in the best way possible. The other person who helped and fought for me from outside without me knowing was Professor Neel B. Gems. He knew about my case and sensed what it was all about. He appeared to treat this as unfair treatment of a foreign national. I felt sure that he had a dialogue with members of my former department. These newly found noble souls were true umpires, my genuine protectors, who enabled my success through fair treatment.

Often, I have speculated, What if I had postponed or cancelled my marriage? I feel certain I would have been allowed to continue with my goal in that earlier field.

***

One day after I returned from a day's study and research in the library, my wife made a justified statement, no doubt in desperation. "How much longer do you think it might take for you to complete your degree?" she asked.

I smiled and responded, "How would you like to have a break and go to New Orleans?" With a big smile, I declared that I had been offered a teaching job as a lecturer in New Orleans.

Part of the urgency, therefore, for accepting a full-time job in New Orleans was the fact that my wife was getting weary of me being a graduate student in eternity, despite the reality of the unjust turn of events. By now, I had been on this campus for four years. On the one hand, the offer of a job duly elevated my status in my new home department at the university. And on the other, it ensured financial security as a lecturer at a prestigious institution in New Orleans. The offer was to my advantage—suitable, self-assuring, and exalting. Not only did it legitimize my pursuit of a desirable profession, but it also propelled me forward as a self-assured scholar.

III

With an appointment letter for a lecturer position in hand, I conferred with my academic adviser at the university about this teaching job, and he did not say anything to discourage me from joining a Black college, as they were known. I must admit that in those days I was not fully mindful of the historical slavery that was practiced in America. Of course, I had read apropos about slavery and the Civil War, but I did not clench how deeply embedded the issue of discriminatory treatment of African American and people of color had continued through perpetuity. Only in the College of Arts at my alma mater did I come across Black students.

If I had been properly educated in social studies and not watched primarily Hollywood fantasy-laden movies, I would have been exposed to America's nation-building from its beginning. I would have known about the following dialogues on race issues:

- Justice John Marshall Harlan inscribed that the White race deems itself to be the dominant race in this country, and so it is in prestige, in achievement, in education, in wealth and in power.
- Harding Coolidge declared that the Divine Providence has not conferred upon any race an exclusive claim on patriotism and character. In fact, America is neither noble nor high-minded

when it comes to treating the colored people. It is the fear of losing privileges that is causing chaos.

- Harry Truman wrote to his fiancé that he believed that Negroes ought to be in Africa, yellow man in Asia, and White man in Europe and America. However, when he became the President, he revised his rhetoric by declaring that all men are created equal and have the right to equal justice under law.

- John F. Kennedy asked a pertinent question: Is there a White man who would change the color of his skin and try to eat lunch in a restaurant, send his children to the best public schools, and vote for the public officials who represent him? He wished all Americans to be able to enjoy life evenly.

- Lynden B. Johnson lamented the legacy of bigotry and injustice. He would have preferred that Black and Brown people in a White society should stand on equal ground. Indeed, it was LBJ who was to change the history of racism, bigotry, and injustice. He guided through the United States Congress a legislation on civil rights.

- Congressman John Lewis, a civil rights pioneer, wished America would overcome hatred, cruelty, and racism. Instead, be known for love, grace, and godliness.

Surely, I realized this job offer at a Black institution in the south was my opportunity to learn about America, and not only prosper in a gainful employment. This Black university was an American institution of higher learning. The concept to educate Black youth was put forth at the 1879 Louisiana State Constitutional Convention. Being a colored person myself, I thought higher education for the African American was a conciliatory idea and was not only a remedy for annihilations suffered by them for centuries. It would not only help improve their life but benefit the whole country in its productive power.

The principle behind the creation of a parallel system of education, one for White and another for Black, was to separate the mixing of the so-called superior White and inferior Black races. In theory the allocation of resources was to be at par, and the product would purportedly equalize citizens for a modern society. But was equality feasible or even possible? A short paradoxical answer has to be in the negative.

When Robert Lane in a seminal piece of his sociological research interviewed a stratified sample of American men, asking them how they would react to real social equality, he received odious answers. Some of the men said equality would be chaotic; the world would collapse. All said equality would deprive them of their goals and incentives in life. Many asked, "What's the point to life if you can't rise above others?" And to excel, there must be inequality, most argued.

Student equity and diversity is a persistent dispute even now. At a recent Palm Beach County (Florida, 2021) School Board meeting, the members and the parents spent three days arguing about removing from a policy statement the phrase, "White advantage" for certain students. Opponents of removing the statement on student equity had harassed board members. They had packed School Board meetings and named anti-racism initiatives as divisive, un-American, Marxist, communist, and Nazi-like. They would favor retaining privileges for White students in public schools. Efforts by the top political leaders to not teach racism in social studies were raising concerns by educators that the State of Florida is trying not only to whitewash slavery but erase other blemishes in American history. Ostensibly, the goal was to stifle efforts to create equity for Black and Brown students.

America's imbedded view on White privileges endures and would be a factor to reckon with for a long time. That has been the prevailing American view. Thus, the first contradiction that I saw was that our enlightened, Hollywood promoted, nation-state ran on obscure practices. This was, and still is, a serious dilemma that America must face. But the answer to inequality has so far escaped this much touted land. And it is not just a grubby fetish. It is a national fascination with differences based on skin color, class, gender, and nationality. It is a Darwinian theme that propels businesses, and for many it makes life worth living. Do we really have to look down on someone, or whoever? Indeed, it is a pitiless basis for life that displays a great deal of fear. It stays in our mind partly because of the conservative fascination with strength over weakness, and a spurious superiority against the forged inferior.

Lane goes further. He reveals that this antagonism to equality arises from a sense of fear. The fear is rationalized. Scholars have shown how this is rationalized out. In the capitalistic view, inequality is useful—it keeps the variety of jobs in our economy staffed. That is the economic point of view. Another view is that it tends to minimize the competition. It is better to have a minimally qualified labor force that could maximize profits for the privileged by reducing their wages.

One of the reasons universities did not encourage their foreign students, as this author, to stay on after their graduation was to exclude them from the labor market. They were told, "You can best serve your people with your advanced education here, and your country needs you!"

***

During the American Civil War, the U.S. Congress created the land-grant colleges using the proceeds of federal land sales, expecting that it would initiate problem-solving research institutions of higher education. My own alma mater was a land-grant university which utilized extra funds to streamline the curricula. The outmoded hackneyed classical education was replaced by functional knowledge that helped improve quality of life, promoted health and safety, along with developing the economy. In 1880, the Louisiana General Assembly chartered a university for the Blacks to be located in Baton Rouge, and when the classes began the following year, it also became a land-grant college.

The Louisiana Constitutional Convention of 1921 authorized the Legislative Act of 1922 that mandated the educational institutions to be improved. As a result, during the next thirty years almost a third of the original buildings on Baton Rouge campus were built. Student enrollment grew from five hundred to nearly ten thousand. Because of the opposition of Louisiana State University Law School (for Whites only) to admit African Americans into its law program, a special Louisiana Convention allowed the formation of Southern University Law Center in 1947.

Southern University was one of the first historically Black colleges to receive visits from First Lady Eleanor Roosevelt in 1943. Thereafter, during 1956 to 1964, this university opened new campuses in New Orleans and Shreveport. I joined the faculty in New Orleans in the fall of 1964.

During the summer of 1964, it did not take exceptionally long for us to pack and head out to New Orleans. The Civil Rights movement was at its peak, and we had to travel through the thick forests of southern United States that were notorious traps for champions of Civil Rights volunteers. We were not in that category, but we felt vulnerable. The week we were driving southward, three Civil Rights workers from the northern states were murdered. Their bodies were not to be found anywhere. Along the way and at our destination, we saw what we had not seen before in the mid-Western states of Missouri, Illinois, Michigan, Iowa, Ohio, and Kansas. There were separate public facilities for Blacks and Whites. It was a freaky setting. We wondered if this was really America, or were there two Americas? Elsewhere, racial discrimination was subtle and sly, but here in the Deep South it was openly and unashamedly practiced. People treated each other based on the color of their skin.

The words Caucasian and White were used interchangeably, and it was meant to emphasize whiteness as a desirable and a superior race. This concept was popularized in the late eighteenth century by a German anthropologist. Switching from skulls to skin, J. Friedrich Blumenbach divided humans into five races of color—White, yellow, copper, tawny, and tawny-Black to jet-Black. He ascribed these differences to climate. Still convinced that people of the Caucasus were the paragons of beauty, Blumenbach placed residents of North Africa and India in the Caucasian category, sliding into a linguistic breakdown based on the common derivation of Indo-European languages.

Thomas Jefferson and Ralph Waldo Emerson suffused Blumenbach's influence, relabeling the category of White as superior. They adopted the

Saxons as their ideal, making Americans as the direct, absolute, and undiluted descendants of the English. Later included in this group were the Germans. In general, Western labels for racial superiority moved thus: Caucasian → Saxon → Teutonic → Nordic → Aryan → White/ Anglo.

In 1889, the original Oxford English Dictionary noted that the term Caucasian had been virtually redundant. But they spoke too soon. Blumenbach's authority had given the word a pseudoscientific patina that preserved its appeal. Even now, the word conveys a treatment of race as a peculiar technocratic gravity.

There is another reason to use the word White, argues Jennifer L. Hochschild, a professor of African American studies at Harvard. She claimed that the court, or some clever clerk, did not really want to use the word White partly because nearly half of Hispanics considered themselves White. The term White turns out to be much more ambiguous than we used to think it was.

There are several terms that refer to various degrees of blackness, both current and out of favor. These are: African American, mulatto, Negro, colored, and octoroon. Comparable options for Whites are not standard. However, in Texas they used Anglo. Growing up during the fight for independence in India, the "Quit India" movement against the British included a word which referred Europeans as "albinos." Protestors on the streets were shouting, "Albinos, go home."

***

In 1803, France sold close to a million square miles of land west of the Mississippi river to the emerging United States of America in a treaty known as the Louisiana Purchase. This acquisition was an implausible deal for the United States; the final cost was less than five cents per acre, or more than five-hundred million dollars in today's currency. Occupied foreign French territory was mainly unexplored wilderness, and so the fertile soils and other valuable natural resources we know about now might not have been factored in the low purchase value at the time.

New Orleans, being the prime real estate of the Louisiana Purchase, became a major port city as well as the largest city in the state. The city was named after the Regent of France. Originally it belonged to the Chitimacha Indian tribes of North America. Most of the surviving architecture of the Vieux Carré (French Quarter) dates from the French period. After the United States acquired the city, it grew rapidly with the influx of new Americans, namely, the French and the Creole people. Sugar and cotton were cultivated with slave labor on large plantations outside the city.

This area was exposed to flooding even before the age of negative elevation. In the late twentieth century, however, scientists and residents gradually became aware of the city's increased vulnerability to swamping. In 1965 when we lived there, Hurricane Betsy caused havoc and killed hundreds of residents, even though the majority of the city remained dry. We watched the approach of this hurricane on television as it finally turned slightly away from a direct hit to where we were. The rain-induced flood demonstrated the weakness of the pumping system. Since that time, measures were taken to refurbish New Orleans' hurricane defenses by enhancing pumping capacity. But that too was not enough as proven by the Katrina disaster of 2005.

***

In 1901, New Orleans saw the opening of a saloon on the edge of the French Quarter and the whole town came to marvel its opulence. It was known as Storyville. Entrepreneur Tom Anderson, of Scotch-Irish descent, went all out to overwhelm people with the décor and blocks of electric light. On Basin Street sophisticated brothels flourished in a multi-story Victorian mansion. Ms. Lulu White, a mixed-race woman, built her own mansion that specialized in interracial sex. The highlight though was a jazz parlor.

A Blue Book published by Anderson included bios and photos of high-class prostitutes annotated with symbols for their race: "C" for colored, "J" for Jewish, "Oct" for octoroon or one-eighth Black, and "W" for White. It was a testimony to New Orleans' diversity and tolerance.

By the late nineteenth century, New Orleans was populated largely by Brazilians, Creoles, French, Germans, Haitians, Scots, Spaniards, former slaves, and by shades of White and Black.

The excitement of Storyville era goes far beyond sex, crime and corruption. By 1905, there were two-hundred and thirty brothels in Storyville that caused continuous battle between the Victorian Anglo-Saxon reformers of the uptown, and the middle-class downtown dwellers who relished permissive mores. The key topic was the awkward relationship of civic reform to class prejudice. Landed gentry and social elite of the uptown were opposed to the tolerance of racial mingling that exemplified Storyville. The uptown intolerance was not about the brothels but about racial intermingling. So, they found a way to punish businesses that allowed all classes. The practice of lynching of both Blacks and Italians ensured that the brothels were earmarked for the privileged class.

As a result, a new class system emerged. The class nuance was interwoven with the emergence of the jazz music. Jazz respected no color line. Hence, this new style of music was not just a diversion, but it retained Storyville's spirit of diversity. On street corners one heard marching brass bands, church spirituals, plantation blues, and the Creole orchestras. Returning Spanish-American War veterans were there, along with ragtime pianists, African drummers, Congo Square dancers, and opera house singers. The first great jazz artist was Buddy Bolden. With his whining cornet he initiated ragging hymns, marches, and dance tunes. He invited well know musicians including Louis Armstrong to join him. All of them played in the clubs of Storyville.

New Orleans in the nineteenth century had been racially progressive, especially for Creoles who were French-speaking Roman Catholics and had intermarried with Europeans. As early as the 1870s, Black people could vote and serve on juries, marriage between different races was legal, and schools, beaches, and many neighborhoods were integrated.

However, the reconstruction era created a new dynamic—a Jim Crow epoch. The so-called reformers of the city passed segregation laws to crack down with moral schemata, especially on prostitution. In

1908, the state legislature passed a bill barring musical performances in saloons and prohibited Blacks and Whites from being served in the same establishment. Women were excluded from the bars altogether. Activities considered sinful by the upper-class elite went underground but were not eradicated.

Besides, when the United States entered World War I, and New Orleans became a military transit area, a federal law was passed that banned prostitution within ten miles of a military encampment. That was the final nail on the coffin of New Orleans' success and the end of commercial class of Storyville. Yet the privileged White elite had a soft heart for jazz. Vice and jazz were twins, along with blackness, and Italian affinity.

Sexual identity is a serious problem in every country. Most societies have informal ways of helping these individuals. Even in New Orleans of those days there arose obscure places where people went for help. They did not just go to these places within the confines of Storyville to procure sex; they went there for counseling. They knew what they sought. Most went there to seek an understanding of their behavior adjustment that depended on physical and psychological factors.

These places of public sex also played an important role in rehabilitating those who were unable to function as normal couples— both married and not married. Becoming aware of sexual feelings is a normal developmental phase of adolescence. Sometimes adolescents have same-sex feelings or experiences that cause confusion about their sexual orientation. This confusion inevitably declines over time, with dissimilar outcomes for atypical individuals. Intersex people are individuals born with any of several variations in sex characteristics including chromosomes, gonads, sex hormones, or genitals that, according to the UN Office of the High Commissioner for Human Rights, do not fit the typical definitions for male or female bodies.

The sex counsellor at these places did not go to graduate schools and earn a psychiatry degree. Instead, they were older experienced men and women who had been in the sex business all their life. Their goal was to help clients figure out their genuine preferences and the life they would choose to live. If they were still confused these experts would simply guide them toward androgyny as a steppingstone to the final settling point. Androgyny is the combination of masculine and feminine characteristics, resulting in an ambiguous form. It may be expressed via biological sex, gender identity, gender expression, and sexual identity.

One finds in Indian mythology many androgynous Gods and Goddesses. For example, *Ardhanarisvara*—the Hindu god Shiva and his consort Parvati—are often shown as a single deity. Sometimes the female form of the god Shiva appears as a female along with all the attributes of the male Shiva. Also, the Hindu god Vishnu, and his consort Lakshmi, appear as a single deity.

***

This city of New Orleans, we were repeatedly advised, was well known for its multicultural and multilingual heritage through its cuisine, architecture, music, and particularly as the birthplace of jazz. The annual Mardi Gras was the highlight of the year. Despite all this, the public places remained segregated.

When we arrived in New Orleans before the start of first semester, we located the apartment that was reserved for us by the officials of the university. All inhabitants there were Blacks and of lower socio-economic background. My wife and I stood out like a sore thumb. Being different from them, we were on display. In fact, whenever anyone visited any of the occupants, we had to come out to meet them. After a while it became very annoying. We objected to it and the manager did not like it. So, we decided to move. We found another apartment complex in the White section of town. It was a great relief. The university dean was apologetic about it and admitted that he did not know where we would have preferred to live. He did not realize that Asian Indians could rent in an all-White community.

We saw how New Orleans was thoroughly segregated racially; restaurants, hotels, hospitals, laundromats, and drugstores had displayed clearly marked signs. Every public facility flashed in bold black letters, "Whites Only," or "For Blacks." Somehow not all colored peoples were classified as Blacks. I went everywhere hesitatingly. But I would normally not be hired at a White university that was purely for White faculty. I assumed that is why I was easily offered a job without a PhD degree at a Black university. This university was a part of the "separate but equal," system of higher education. Euphemistically, it was both separate but unequal as far as the funding was concerned. There was a shortage of qualified faculty for sure, primarily because of disparity in funding.

And we watched how by Christmas, or within four months of our arrival, all these signs at public facilities disappeared in the wake of President L. B. Johnson's Civil Rights legislation that Congress had finally passed into law. It was fascinating to observe the physical transformation of this city. But did it change people's attitudes and behavior? Not at all. Much more needed to be done to reach an acceptable level of civility. After LBJ's Civil Rights legislation came into force two White students, led by my wife, filed a friendly suit against the university and brought about the racial integration of that Black campus. No more was Southern University system a legally segregated institution of higher learning for the African Americans. Students of all races could now enroll and attend classes.

After settling in our preferred apartment in New Orleans, my wife looked for a job to keep her occupied. She found a suitable one at a major hospital in downtown New Orleans. As a formidable hospital it lived up to its name, serving one of the largest populations of indigent citizens in the United States. In its mission, it was second only to Bellevue Hospital in New York City, the largest continually run hospital with more than 2,600 beds. Its trauma center was second only to Cook County Hospital in Chicago. Simultaneously, it was a teaching hospital for the local universities.

My wife was hired as the head nurse of a forty-bed non-acute neurology unit. It was not a big deal because she was the only RN with ample experience. The rest of the staff on all their shifts was Licensed

Vocational Nurses (LVN) and nursing assistants. The staff at this hospital was exclusively African American.

All the in-patient floors in this hospital were separated by race, the two east wings being Black, and the two west wings being White, each with a head nurse. There were nursing supervisors for each floor for both wings. The head nurses like my wife rotated to relieve the supervisors on weekends.

One weekend my wife had coffee with the head nurse of the other unit on Seven West. This nurse told my wife, "I don't have anything against integration but what if they get the blood mixed up?" My wife was flabbergasted that this professionally trained registered nurse really believed that there were racial differences in human blood. Innocently, the locally trained nurse tried to be virtuous and unbiased, but she was a born and bred southern girl with all its baggage of ignorance and misguided racial prejudices.

That afternoon when my wife prepared to make rounds on the West Unit, she was warned by a distressed nurse to expect something different. My wife had learned that there would be a new admission in the men's White ward. As she made her rounds that afternoon, she met the new patient. Comfortably settled in his bed there was indeed a Black gentleman. No one, especially the other White patients, appeared concerned.

Apparently, the hospital was planning its strategy for carrying out integration as mandated by the Civil Rights Act of 1964. At the other hospitals where my wife worked, further north, the White and Black patients were routinely put together as beds became available without giving a thought to their race. Of course, it was different in the Deep South. In southern parts of the United States social and cultural norms were entirely different. By and large, they remain so even now, and a de facto racial segregation continues to be experienced. Racial prejudices were rampant there and the Whites did not want to treat the Blacks as equal. It was all about the fear of impending equality—a system in which the underprivileged classes could not compete for the available prime jobs.

My adaptation to the culture of this Black college was smooth. All my colleagues with whom I shared office space had been educated in the northeast and, therefore, they had met other Indian scholars. I found them cordial and helpful in finding my way around. Sociology instructors were uniquely frank about the Black-White variances in the southern United States. They informed me that many Blacks, the way they looked, could pass as White people because of miscegenation. Therefore, they would move to the predominantly White northern states to settle down.

During the academic year I was at this institution, I learned firsthand from my colleagues about the disparity that invariably affected their lives daily. Resilience, I was told repeatedly, is what the American societal norms infused into its colored citizens. It taught them to tolerate racial prejudice, endure harassment, accept marginalization, and never expect privileges that are normal for the dominant class. These differential treatments ended up causing them post-traumatic stress disorder (PTSD). Constant anxiety created a syndrome of high blood pressure and early death. And yet so many of them tried hard and succeeded.

They succeeded because they did not expect too much. They were expected to, "suck it up and move on." On the positive side, it enabled them to accept things as they were, and they did their best to achieve success by learning not to feel pity on themselves. Mindfully coping with the hurdles and disappointments caused by the cultural imperatives, the Black people continued to do their duty in an utterly relegated environment without ignoring what was going on with their central nervous system. Remaining focused on their goal they became fully functional human beings despite repeated setbacks.

During winter semester, I accompanied two sociology professors to the annual conference of the American Sociological Association that was held at Duke University in Durham, North Carolina. The keynote speaker was none other than Dr. Martin Luther King Jr. who spoke on the struggles and promises of Civil Rights movement in America. He received a standing ovation and at the end all of us lined up to shake hands with him. When I approached him, he smiled and extended his hands. He referred to his trip to India and reminded me that Gandhi's campaign of non-violent disobedience had proven useful for oppressed and powerless people there and here.

Gandhi was a practicing Hindu. He studied the Gita and the Bible daily. For him, the Sermon on the Mount was the essence of Jesus's teaching. He proclaimed that Jesus was one of the prodigious teachers of mankind. Gandhi taught his followers about the Beatitudes and God's laws. He practiced what he taught; by praying, by giving, and by fasting. To Gandhi the promise of righteousness was for this life right here and now, neither for the future, nor in our next life. And so, we must live our lives in accordance with the divine teachings. Those teachings were also the fountain of his campaign to seek the ouster of an alien rule that kept his people in bondage.

With the tools of morality and justice at their disposal, for both Gandhi and King, the challenge was to achieve self-rule and a modicum of civic equality, respectively. When there is a crushing power to deal with there is no conceivable recourse but to cultivate an attitude of love—love thy enemy. In this way, the oppressor is adulated for its amiability, and you win the game by escaping the status quo. In case of India, the British colonial leaders were asked to stay on and help make the transition to self-rule possible. And in case of the African Americans in the United States, the aim was to endow them with civil rights.

Mahatma Gandhi did not consider the British as enemy. Similarly, MLK was not anti-White. Because they were deeply religious men, they did not think in terms of "us" and "them." Believers of any religion are governed by the laws of nature that regulates our humanity. For them non-dual consciousness is the natural state. We are all different in appearance and functioning but connected at the source. That in essence is going "beyond religion."

***

More than a million Black people migrated from the South to northern cities throughout the early decades of the twentieth century. With meagre funds and scarce job opportunities, the new arrivals were forced to rent inferior housing that lacked clean water and sewer lines. Unsanitary living conditions caused their certain death from tuberculosis and the flu at about twice the rates of White people. Black women ended up dying three times more than White women from childbirth, and woefully Black newborns lived three fewer years than White babies.

What has been going on for hundreds of years is the systematic neglect of Black Americans. In 2018, they died at higher age-adjusted rates than White people from nine of the top fifteen causes of death. There needs to be a major wholesale change in the future. The disparities in public health require a commonsense approach. Persistent inequality in America is not just due to physical factors, or genetics. It is due to socio-cultural imperatives.

Usually, people point out the genetics and their individual predicament. Certainly, it is not genetics. Black people's income, education and behavior do explain away some of the differences, but not all of it. The real issue is the pervasive structural racism of America that bars them from receiving their fair share of proper life. That is the real cause of their poverty and deplorable living conditions.

Tracing the origins of Black health disparities, we can go all the way back to the slave traders' barracoons. Historians have estimated that at least half of the Africans who were captured and brought to America died before they could be sold as slaves. That was a case of total neglect.

The Covid-19 pandemic has further revealed that Black people are three times more likely than White people to contract the coronavirus, six times more likely to be hospitalized as a result, and twice as likely to die of it. The discrepancy in Black and White infections has become part of a conversation during pandemic about how deeply racism is embedded in the day-to-day lives of Black people. This new epidemic has displayed, in a brief period, what has been the pattern for centuries. Inadequate health insurance for the Black, Brown, and other minorities has resulted in their disproportionately higher rates of infection and death.

All these inequities are endemic to this nation's political economy, and selective predations—stolen land of the Native Americans and the unpaid wages of the African Americans. Those maneuvers have enabled the privileged few capitalists to stash away the lion's share of America's wealth.

While protesting the excessive police brutality, compassionate White marchers have supported Black demonstrators. They have finally understood what the downtrodden have been saying for years. It remains to be seen whether these good White citizens will continue to address the racial prejudice inherent in economic inequality caused by America's lop-sided law enforcement, skewed public policies, and deficient health care.

***

As far as the students at Southern University were concerned, I found most of them to be serious learners, although it was not uncommon to find a few from the rich families who were not fully committed to staying on this campus longer than necessary. Their plan was to move out of state. In writing term papers, these students encountered serious challenges. Therefore, I had to discontinue that requirement, replacing it with an oral class presentation. Ten percent of my students earned an "A" grade, and an equal number failed the courses.

In addition to myself, there were two other Indian professors on campus, one in biology and another in the chemistry department. They did help me adjust on this campus. Dr. Praja was a veterinarian, and in addition to teaching, he managed his own veterinary clinic. Since he had a boat, we went out fishing at least twice a week in nearby lake Ponchatrane. Fishing was good there. At times, I was able to pull up multiple trout from the lake. Sometimes we caught flounders; especially as we got closer to the Gulf of Mexico. Our indoor cat was well fed as a result.

That cat had travelled with us in our Volkswagen beetle all the way to New Orleans. Although well fed, she became ill and we handed her over to Dr. Praja, the veterinarian. He apologized when he could not save that cat. But he provided a replacement that looked just like the deceased one.

In addition to having a comfortable life in New Orleans, I worked diligently and prepared my courses thoroughly. At this university, in addition to my focus areas of comparative government and international relations, I was assigned to teach courses in American government and legislative process.

One day the dean called me to his office and shared his idea about launching a student paper. Since I had a degree in journalism from India, he argued, I should offer a course in journalism and publish a school paper. I took that task and taught students to be reporters and news writers in preparation for publishing the college newspaper. We had a campus wide contest that helped us chose the title. The result was the publication of the first edition of a student newspaper. It was a hit. I recall that the chair of social sciences was openly jealous. As others congratulated me, he made a sarcastic remark. But most pleased was the dean. That is what counted the most. When the time came for contract renewal I was promoted to Assistant Professor.

To reiterate, the faculty who had completed their PhD's, were trained in northern universities. The dean recruited new faculty while they were still working on their graduate degrees. I was in that category too. Later, I learned that several faculty members became awfully cozy in their laidback lifestyle. They stayed on and did not complete their degrees. Because they had a secure job, there was no reason to go back to their alma mater and complete their dissertation. I became very alarmed about this and having experienced the challenges I overcame; I vowed that I would not let that happen to me. But it almost did, especially after receiving a new contract with promotion.

I had no way of judging the seriousness, either of the faculty, or of students. But I knew from my own experience what ought to be the quality of instruction, the credentials, and the ethical conduct of the instructional faculty. Students on this campus were not from the general population. They did not represent diversity. Yet the instructors were doing their job as prescribed and they maintained a rapport owing largely to the firmness of the dean of this campus.

A sociology department colleague whose office was next to mine warned me in the beginning about certain narcissistic young coeds who were crafty. These coeds felt that if a male instructor thought she was sexy that she might earn a better grade in the class. I was told, "They will come to your office with the pretext of asking questions regarding the day's lecture, but they would wear low cut blouses, or be braless, to say the least." Once, I was visited by a young coed who came to flash her fully grown, young breast, but she had no questions. I did not utter a word either.

***

At the conclusion of my first term teaching at Southern University my wife and I flew to Mexico City for a much-delayed vacation. It was a thoroughly exhilarating experience from the time we landed to our departure. Upon landing when we came down the plane on the tarmac there was a photographer taking our photos. It was in fact an incredibly unique experience. Travelling abroad to Mexico was the first time in our rather thorny and wobbly married life that we were out of the country on a pseudo vacation-cum-honeymoon. We seemed to be enjoying ourselves for the first time since the day of our marriage three years ago. In Mexico City, we were treated as dignitaries wherever we went. Could it be that I resembled a native Mexican elite who might be visiting home with a foreign wife?

Our weeklong trip to Mexico City was made possible with the encouragement of my wife's optometrist. He had me come to his office for an eye examination. I did not wear glasses in those days and did not need any prescription from him. Yet, he checked my eyesight and talked to me at length regarding his conversation with my wife about the merit of a trip to Mexico City. I was interested in what he had to say. He told me about the Delta airline flight, the hotel where he and his wife stayed, and the taxi to hire. In fact, we followed his itinerary in the fullest.

We hired that same taxi at the airport and our driver became our guide as well for the week. It was his own car and a livelihood for this man who spoke good English. From the airport he dropped us at our hotel at supper time and said we would start our sightseeing in the morning. It was comforting to know that he was known by the hotel desk clerk.

The hotel was neat and clean, and the staff seemed very efficient. We could call it an old boutique hotel in a residential district that had an impressive Mayan décor. Our room, a suite, was attractive and comfortable. That evening we explored the hotel and elected to have dinner in its restaurant before retiring for the evening.

The following morning, the driver showed up with his car at the hotel at 10 AM. I do not remember seeing too many tourists in that hotel. The driver suggested a few places we could go, and I said let us begin visiting important sites in the city.

Mexico City offered countless archaeological sites, and one of the world's largest town squares, the zócalo, filled with Aztec history. We saw the Independence Monument which was a unique blend of colonial and modern architecture of Paseo de la Reforma. Then, we visited Chapultepec Park which included the Mexican president's residence, a large zoo, several museums, and an amusement park.

When the sun set, we went to the forty-fifth floor of the World Trade Center which had a panoramic view of the City. The following day we listened to a mariachi band at Garibaldi Plaza. Another day we went to the ancient floating gardens of Xochimilco. We enjoyed a thoroughly exotic scene there that made me ask where I was, Mexico or Thailand.

On the fourth day, we travelled to the mammoth Pyramids of the Sun and the Moon. The neighboring countryside was sprawling with grey bushes. It was the highlight of one of the largest pre-Columbian cities in the Americas. But the most spectacular was the Plumed Serpent.

We had an early start for the long trip northeast to climb around in the morning, and during the mid-day sun we took shelter in the museum. It was not easy to cover that entire historic place in a day but at least we saw the highlights of the area.

On the fifth day we travelled to Cuernavaca, just 50 miles from Mexico City. It seemed like a long trip because of uneven roads and balmy weather. Unlike the mile-high Mexico City, Cuernavaca was a place of rest and recreation. Aztec emperors, conquistadors, princesses, artists, and many foreign retirees chose to live there. I remember it as the center of silver mines.

The following day we explored our hotel neighborhood in Mexico City and found some thrilling sights, including a farmer's market where I could not resist buying luscious ripe mangoes. I enjoyed all five of them in our hotel room that afternoon. That evening, I suffered from stomachache. We were not supposed to drink tap water and I used that to wash the mangoes.

Mexican cuisine is as complex as any of the praised cuisines in the world such as those of India, Italy, France and Greece. It is created mostly with ingredients native to Mexico as well as those brought over by the Spanish invaders.

The debate, however, continues about how much Mexican food is still indigenous and how much is European. Yet, the basis of their diet is still corn and beans with chili pepper as a seasoning. Genuine Mexican food is spicy and hot. So is the Indian food. Yet, in my estimate they are diametrically different in taste and flavor. It took me some time to relish the Mexican spices. For my taste, though, nothing can replace the inevitable curry dishes. My favorite food will remain the predictable rice and dal.

To end our visit to Mexico, on the final day we visited the Metropolitan Cathedral of the Assumption of Mary of Mexico City. It is the oldest and largest Roman Catholic cathedral in the Americas and the center of the Roman Catholic Archdiocese of Mexico.

The cathedral was built in sections from 1573 to 1813 around the original church that was constructed soon after the Spanish conquest. It depicted the Gothic cathedrals of Spain. Although a solid foundation was laid for the Cathedral, the soft clay soil it was built on has been a threat to its structural integrity. We spent half a day there exploring mostly the inside. It felt like a peaceful holy ground.

Outside was a huge main square, or plaza. This plaza was in the heart of the historic center of Mexico City. It used to be known simply as the "Main Square" or "Arms Square." Today its formal name is Plaza de la Constitución (Constitution Square).

We saw worshippers in various stages of their crawl toward the entrance of the Cathedral. It was painful to watch them go through the self-inflicted agony and pain. Relatives and friends were behind them praying as the worshipper crept his or her way toward the entrance.

It was a thoroughly enlightening, refreshing, and educational trip to Mexico. We talked to friends and relatives about this trip for an awfully long time. And some of our friends borrowed this page from our life's story.

***

Like Mexico City, New Orleans too was an enchanting place. It was a tourist town, especially for those interested in a hop over to Mexico as we did. *How could we afford such a trip?* My university salary provided us a reasonably comfortable life—restaurant, fishing, travels, and entertainment were affordable. People in New Orleans were fun-loving; they appreciated parties, and organized festivals such as the Mardi Gras parade.

Mardi Gras was celebrated with music, picnics, floats, exhibitions, and for us it was yet another holiday in New Orleans! During this festival everyone wore colorful clothes—purple, green, and gold—adorned with long beads caught from the decorated floats. People sat on the curves throwing foam balls, playing music, and not only having a picnic, but watching the crowds walk by between parades.

The raucous Mardi Gras parades with riders on elaborate floats tossed trinkets to adoring throngs. We were at the parade one day on

Canal Street and saw some of the weirdest scenes: a girl received a coconut from a man on a float only when she uncovered her breasts. The reason for this display was that during Mardi Gras the coconuts were a great treasure and hard to find. That incident happened again whenever colorful beads were thrown at young women. Some women did anything to get what they wanted from those riding the floats.

Tradition required that young women assembled on Bourbon Street should at a minimum bare their breasts, better they throw their bras at the men on floats in exchange for a handful of beads. I could not believe what I was watching in amazement. *Could someone account for this?* Some say that this was never and is still not a tradition. Saying it was a tradition is like saying that people who get drunk and pass out on Bourbon Street are following tradition as well! This does not occur everywhere in New Orleans even during Mardi Gras, just on selected Street in the French Quarter. It is an area known for its strip joints where those interested in this sort of exhibition can witness it year-round.

On some late nights, a parade for adults started on one end of the Bourbon Street. Women and men in this X-rated parade were not fully clothed. Participants in the parade were heavily tattooed, especially in their upper part of the body. It was not uncommon to spot women with pierced rings hanging from their nostrils and nipples. The charming balconies in the French Quarter were delightful places to have dinner. Once we enjoyed the atmosphere of the area as the sounds of jazz below drifted by while we ate. Our dinner on one of the Bourbon Street balconies during Mardi Gras was an experience to remember. The French Quarter at night during Mardi Gras, however, was not anyone's idea of a good time because of drunken lunkheads roaming the streets. People misbehaved. One should just visit the market early in the day when the street musicians, artists, and families enjoyed the sights in safety. The Riverwalk was lovely, and people were savoring their walk. Mardi Gras was and always has been a family event. It was not for drunks, and misbehavior was never tolerated. It is sad that so many have violated the meaning of this celebration.

Unfortunately, Mardi Gras was generally viewed in terms of fun activities in the French Quarter, i.e., flashing women, tourists who got drunk, the crowd surging, and a spring break horde pushing others aside to catch a glimpse of the parade! The locals declared, "This is not Mardi Gras, and it has absolutely nothing to do with the *real* Mardi Gras celebration." Unfortunately, sex makes ready-made news. So, every news cameraman visiting this beautiful city during Mardi Gras headed for the spring break crowd on Bourbon Street. The result was that the storekeepers who had disbursed thousands of dollars and months of time planning and decorating their store fronts were left out. Their business did not get the exposure it deserved and did not fully benefit.

Mardi Gras has always been celebrated in this predominantly Catholic city on the eve of Ash Wednesday. That is when Christians receive ashes and begin forty days of sacrifice in imitation of *Our Lord*, ending at Easter when everyone celebrates the Resurrection! It is amazing how a sacred and religious event has been turned partially into a filthy facet of human existence; indeed, it depicted American hedonism itself.

***

By the middle of the academic year, I was getting used to my good carefree life and an easy teaching job. This life of luxury made me uncomfortable. It made me very edgy because this job for me was supposed to be just a diversion, a break. So, I began to think of returning to my alma mater to complete the doctorate degree. I wrote letters to several of my angelic professors I had gotten to know well, including my academic adviser. They all wrote back and said I must return. One professor wrote, "What are you doing there?" Following letters were profoundly important and meaningful to me and therefore are reproduced below.

The first letter was from a very delightful human being, a professor in the sociology-anthropology department, Dr. Neal B. Gems, from whom I had taken two courses. He expressed gratitude for me for sending along a listing of the courses that I had completed. He asked:

If you apply for a pre-doctoral fellowship, I shall be pleased to write a letter in your behalf. You have a very good record. Also, I will be glad to look over your outline for the proposed PhD research project. I had not heard from you or about you since I returned from abroad, so was pleased to know your present location. Are you teaching at the university there? I do not seem to recognize this university. Is it a new one?

The next letter was from another professor of mine, Dr. Robert Kenberry, who taught the American Government class and for a semester I was his research assistant. He wrote to me from Calcutta, India, where he was a Fulbright visiting scholar. He wrote:

I was glad to receive both your letters. We have been on a long puja holiday since October 4 and so your letter of the 10th did not reach me until yesterday, when my classes resumed at the university. Mail reaches me most quickly at the residence address above.

First let me congratulate you on the successful summer with the Inter-University Consortium—a first rate outfit as you have doubtless found out—and on your position at the university there. You probably would not wish to stay there permanently, but I have known some excellent scholars there and it seems to have a good reputation.

As for your plans for the pre-doctoral research project, the title alone is exciting, and doubtless you would dig up some fascinating hypotheses out of the data. When you get a tentative outline let me see it.

My wife and I have been enjoying India immensely. There are serious problems challenging those in government—getting more serious I believe, month by month. The government and leading citizens are rising to the need, but the big question repeatedly comes up—will the tempo of solutions keep pace with the mounting problems.

I have been fortunate in getting around quite a bit, mostly in connection with USIS and its various university programs. These university communities are keenly interested in USA and world problems, and I have not yet had a single hostile encounter.

Please write again when you have time, telling me a little more of your ideas for the research. I'll help you in any way I can, though as you know you are far more versant with the application of behavioral tools to sophisticated research patterns than I. Very best wishes to you and your wife.

Dr. R. Dawle, Vice Chair of the Research Center, who later employed me, was a methodologist and an excellent lecturer. He was a great motivator for me in my research endeavors. He was pleased that I was finding my job in New Orleans enjoyable and finding New Orleans to be a delightful city. He continued:

As I suggested to you last summer, there would appear to be a good chance of obtaining foundation support for your dissertation research. You may be correct in assuming that application by a faculty member for support of your research interests would improve the chances for financial assistance. On the other hand, if an application were made to the Social Science Research Council, it would have to be made by you.

Whatever procedure is followed, it will be necessary for you to write a brief, but tightly reasoned, prospectus of your proposed dissertation research. You should clearly set forth the focus of your research, the framework you intend to employ, the relation between your project and pertinent work that has been done by other social scientists, and the methods of data collection you intend to employ.

Once you complete the prospectus, we can then move rather quickly to a decision as the most likely sources of financial support, and to a determination as to whether an application should be made by you or by some member of the faculty.

In the meantime, I shall check our collection of foundation annual reports to see which might be the most appropriate source of funds for your project.

Best of luck. I shall look forward to receiving your prospectus and am hopeful that we can persuade some foundation of the wisdom of supporting the kind of research you have in mind.

By far the most important letter was from Professor D. Ward, my primary adviser, who was later the main guiding light toward completing the Doctor of Philosophy degree. He was probably the youngest professor who was not only thoughtful but sincere about the pace of progress for his students. His letter began with a word of advice:

If you are thinking of returning to Columbia next year, I would urge you to apply for a teaching assistantship. With the experience you are gaining this year, I should think you would have a very good chance of gaining assistantship. This would enable you to prepare for your comprehensive examination and, if successful in that endeavor, to begin the groundwork for your dissertation. Then, should you be successful in applying for a research grant, you would be able to move swiftly to the dissertation's completion. I realize that this will seem like a rather lengthy postponement of the degree, but I think that, given the fact that you have not yet completed all stages before the dissertation, it would be unrealistic to expect to begin work on that project early next year.

I hope the teaching experience is an enjoyable one and that you are finding your new role suitable to your tastes and capacities. The first few years of teaching are full of frustrations, as I well know, but if an occasional feeling of satisfaction reaches you there is no real cause of concern. Again, I apologize for my delay in answering. I hope it will not have inconvenienced you.

The above letters were instrumental in my final decision to return to my alma mater and resume my endeavors toward completing the requirements for my doctorate degree. Despite this, the task of extricating myself from this university was not going to be easy. I had already been given a teaching contract for the following year and promoted to assistant professor. The answer to my egress came when I talked to a colleague in another department who was much closer to the dean. "You do not have to see the dean," she advised. "Just write a nice letter and leave. I will take care of the rest."

When we arrived back on our own grounds, we rented an apartment slightly away from the campus which required driving to campus for both of us. The department that facilitated my return was more welcoming, in that I had given up a fulltime teaching job and was there for completing requirements for the doctorate degree. My adviser had me enroll in research courses and helped me focus on preparing for my comprehensive examinations. On my own, I chose to audit courses also.

Formally, I was employed by the Research Center as an assistant. My supervisor, Dr. Dawle, gave me research assignments that simply complemented my studies and research endeavors toward a doctoral dissertation. He was the most congenial person around; genteel, articulate, and graceful.

Near the end of the first semester my comprehensive examinations were scheduled. To do a good job answering questions scrupulously required four to six-hours for each of the four written sessions. Questions given to me were in the areas of comparative government, international relations, methodology, and sociology as an ancillary field. It took four different sessions for writing answers to questions in four subject areas. Soon thereafter, an oral examination was held on the same subjects by a committee of four professors. Their questions were designed to judge my analytical skills and not on affirming their political persuasions as in a previous department. Being genuine scholars, they clearly separated knowledge from their personal vistas.

I was successful in answering all their questions and hence declared acceptable. I passed. Truly, I had never felt so ecstatic before. I was euphoric with my own performance! It equipped me with an utter sense of self-confidence. At last, I was home, so to say. In fact, when I went back to the apartment and gave the good news to my wife in the living room, I jumped so high in my ecstasy that I almost hit the ceiling! Later in the week that same room had to witness the arrival of a color TV—a real material recompense for my efforts in the form of a conspicuous consumption. Hard labor must be followed by a blissful joyous ecstasy! Now I will not be walking a mile to the Student Common to watch the Six O'clock news on NBC by Huntley-Brinkley.

Following my celebrated success, I walked around the campus with my head held high. I took my beaming face and puffed-up ego to the Student Union, hoping I might run into someone from the days of malaise. But I did not. It was better that way. As I settled down some serious thinking had to go into finalizing my research project for a seminal dissertation that until now was in its embryonic stages.

Being on the staff of the Research Center, I began to interact with some of the younger PhD's, notably a scholar who had just joined the staff and his specialty was survey research. We explored the scope of my research topic, discussed the literature associated with it, pondered over the methodology to be utilized, and strategies to pursue for collecting field data. What emerged was a sixty-four-item survey instrument designed to study socio-political attitudes and the policy tracks concerning modernization in India. Having designed numerous such instruments, this competent specialist at the Center helped me give the final touches to a questionnaire protocol. Now, the challenge was to take it out to the field in India, do a test run, make necessary modifications, duplicate the questionnaire, and collect the final data.

My supervisors and I discussed the matter of making applications for a grant. But that would take time. Given the urgency, I decided to travel to India as soon as possible for testing the instrument and collecting the field data myself.

IV

During the summer of 1966, I boarded a fanjet airplane in New York City and arrived in Mumbai via London at a cost of four-hundred dollars roundtrip. It was a charter flight; the passengers were all expatriates, along with a scattering of college-age American tourists. In India, I lived with friends and relatives for close to two months. To begin the dissertation project in Mumbai, I stayed with my former house mate, Maniar, from the American campus. He was helpful in duplicating and collating my survey instrument. He helped in assembling an array of respondents to interview and try out my survey protocol. As a result, I made few changes. With a final interview document in hand, I went to Delhi and to towns in central and eastern India. Given the distance, time, and shortage of funds, I had to mail the survey protocol to several willing experts in the field. One source of help came from my brother who had drawn together a cadre of contacts directly involved in various aspects of development projects in central India.

While I was getting my questionnaire duplicated at a printing shop near Mumbai's India gate, I noticed a huge crowd across the street at a restaurant. One of the technicians told me that this event takes place every day during lunch hour when this restaurant partakes in a cabaret show for office workers. They come for a quick lunch, and it costs them twice as much. It is an imitation of what happens in the West. It is a faux adult entertainment usually held in a high society nightclub at a restaurant while the audience eats and drinks. There was neither a theme nor a mood of a cabaret performance, but a trick to attract more gullible customers who cannot afford to miss a fad. I too was curious. So, I walked toward the restaurant, though not recognized to sit at a table. There were none available. I saw a girl who was dressed as a native Adivasi wearing a colorful skirt, a long-sleeve blouse with ample garments, and beaded flowers. There was no bare skin except for her toes because she had no shoes. She was swaying lightly and lip singing a Bollywood song. The audience was enjoying and cat calling so loudly that more people gathered, and the traffic cops arrived to disperse them all.

Unlike this lunch time cabaret, the evening entertainment at posh restaurants in Mumbai had come to define a particular musical genre. It drew on the aesthetics of the decadent, risqué German Weimar-era blended cabarets, burlesque, and vaudeville shows with the stylings of post-1960s hippy music.

Here in India, they had combined the burlesque, which takes place in a theater on stage, with a cabaret which is performed in a nightclub. The contents may have been similar at one time, with perhaps more comics in burlesque, and extra singers/dancers in cabaret.

In selected restaurant, stripping was client focused because they were exclusive clubs for the rich professional elite. Although the girls were performing as strippers, they also wanted to create a one-on-one experience with favorite clients—patrons who paid enormously well. However, in the front part of the restaurant it was a stage show, involving burlesque dancers—focus being on glitter, feathers, and exotic dance.

How India had changed since I lived here until 1957. It seemed India had returned to the Western ways with a vengeance, this time for themselves without the Europeans barring them from entering. Ironically, when burlesque originated in the seventeenth century Italy, where the primary intention of entertainment was in the form of a joke, mockery, and ridicule, it was to teach the audience a moral lesson— drawing their attention toward a social theme. Rather than a straight operatic act, it was an edifying art, and surely an exposure to fables, parables of Jesus, and religious commentary.

As I travelled to the center of the country, I met my younger siblings and at one point we were staying at a hotel. I noticed how caring they were; affection was oozing out of them for their long absent brother. During mealtime on that Monday evening, we realized that it was a non-chapatti day. We will not be eating bread because of Prime Minister Shastri's edict. There was a shortage of wheat in the country. So, my older brother went to talk to the manager, who agreed that because I was from America, I will be served bread. After delivering chapattis to our room, the manager had our doors closed. Therefore, we all had our regular meals together, with bread.

Upon arrival in India in 1966, it became necessary for me to augment another agenda that took an added urgency. Since my departure for Canada in 1957, it was my first family reunion. My drawn-out stay abroad, unintended at first, created a great deal of misunderstanding and ill will. Upon arrival it was obvious that I needed to mend fences. Likewise, but more pressing, was the necessity to procure data for my PhD dissertation research, which had justified the trip in the first place. While in India, I remained on the payroll of the College of Arts and Sciences of my alma mater. So, I could not slack off. As the work on data collection was progressing, simultaneously, I was engaged in healing the estrangements with my mother and older brothers that had pervaded during my long absence of nine years.

Major choices on my part that caused them stress were: first, when I decided to travel from Canada to the United States to continue my studies, and second, when I decided to get married. During this visit, I was becoming especially conscious of my obligations and, therefore, I earnestly tried to appease my mother and older brothers for being gone for a justified reason. Gradually, they realized that I had no choice in the matter because they too wanted me to pursue at all outlays an advanced graduate degree in the United States. They had, however, no idea that in the absence of substantial personal funds I had to work part-time to afford to live as a married graduate student. Besides, I had to seek employment on a different campus as a lecturer for a year. So, the timetable for finishing a degree was stretched. Also, my mentors in India had misinformed me about how long it took to complete a PhD degree in America. Moreover, we have no control of our destiny, do we?

When I had decided to move from Canada to the USA, my oldest half-brother had told my mother and the brother younger to him that I was not telling the whole story. Of course, that was not the truth. Perhaps the reason he claimed innocence was to free himself from his role in my long stay abroad. No doubt, he wanted to minimize his part in pushing me for a foreign education— travelling abroad and pursuing a PhD degree. He put together a claim speciously to abate his role in my long absence.

The ups and downs of my life were not a common episode. As a matter of fact, it was a serendipitous occurrence. All through my stay in North America, through thick and thin, in good times and bad times, I had continued to write letters to India to share major events in my life. What made me do that was a uniquely appeasing upbringing, and the way we always kept in touch with our base. To a degree it was the closeness and care that I had personally experienced growing up under the tutelage of my older brother that had bonded us, especially after the premature death of our father. It was important for me to share with them my decision to marry an overseas woman. I could have kept it to myself as my compatriots suggested. But I thought it was necessary to convey my allegiance to the family, not only with my mother and older brothers, but the younger grown-up siblings as well.

During my visit in 1966, wherever I went and whoever I met, the odor of that discord flashed across my mind and theirs. Except my mother, however, no one mentioned any source of discord. They must have realized that favorable or not, at least I shared the news and came for a visit. Most people in my situation would not, and did not, care to visit their homeland.

For readers benefit it is fitting that I reveal the gist of those dialogues pertaining to my impending marriage. What are being described below are the true but abbreviated contents of letters from my mother, older brothers, sister-in-law, and a younger brother. The emotions expressed therein were also the content of our one-on-one dialog. The very first letter came from my mother who wrote:

> I am writing under duress…my eyes are failing me. I did not think that you would not care about your younger brothers—their education and expenses. It seems you have given up any thought of them. If others had done like this . . . what then? Certainly, you will deceive me by marrying there. What will the people here say?
>
> There are good, educated girls here too; you take my advice, marry when you come here. Here there are good girls too. Your oldest brother is angry that you had told him that you were going for one year, but you have stayed away so long. Now you come back. Will you come back when I am dead? I am writing this letter with pain and anguish. You are disrespecting the names of your father and mine. What a reputation he has had! What will everybody think about you, you yourself are intelligent to know? What effect will it have on your brothers? Only my heart knows how much I long for you, but you do not care. The one who bears and nurtures a son knows only what it is to lose. I am writing thoughtfully.
>
> Now it depends upon you. You may not have even considered how my expenses are met. I know nothing. Now you come back. It seems you have no love for people here. That is why you are still there. Now you come back very soon. I am usually very unwell. When your letter arrived, I was deeply sorry to have read it. I am writing this letter not with any rancor—one tries to make her son understand. You shall not mind me

writing this way. You will understand it yourself. With
my love.

After the death of our father, my oldest brother was our guardian
and counselor, as stated earlier. When he received my letter about my
plans he did not respond, and the brother younger to him did not react
to the news right away. Perhaps they did not think a response was
warranted. But others did immediately. In addition to my mother, they
all communicated the same views of disapproval.

The essence of the letter from my second older brother, KBK,
which arrived much later was equally vigorous. Presumably after much
reflection, KBK explained to me logically the consequences of marrying
someone from a different culture, especially how it would affect the
dynamics of a joint family and its old-fashioned customs and traditions.

> We are not yet advanced to easily face new circumstances.
> Our oldest brother's daughter is now of marriageable age
> and if obstacles arise toward that goal because of your
> missteps, it will certainly shock us. It will be impossible
> that our relatives, extended family, and society will
> accept us. If it is at all possible you should return just as
> you went there, all alone.
>
> Staying for such a long time and not receiving a PhD
> will make everything worthless. You must complete
> it before returning. And, if for some reason you have
> made a mistake of some kind to let us know. We can
> create an environment and guide you properly.

Repeatedly he urged me to make it clear, in plain language, as to
what my plans were. Prolonged stay abroad will mean that when I
return, I will face problems. There will not be a job waiting for me. My
overage will not qualify me for a permanent government job. Even if I
obtained a decent job in India, that would not be adequate to maintain

an acceptable living standard, especially with a foreign wife. He advised me to think of all these matters in depth. He persisted that there is no rush for anything.

Here two points he raised are worth noting. One, he said I would not be able to afford a foreign wife in India. Two, since I have stayed away this long, I should finish my PhD. In closing he wanted me to know that we shared the same blood and that they think only of my happiness. Bravo and Amen!

In all his innocence and naiveté one of my younger brothers, whom I would call MB, ventured to persuade me that because of the urgency to educate him this is the right time for me to return. He made sure that as a younger brother it would not be appropriate, indeed considered insolence, to comment on my plans to marry abroad. Yet, MB did object:

> You have every right to get married as you please, but you must think of certain matters. You must set a good example for your younger brothers, nephews, and nieces. Otherwise, the effect of your decision could likely be that I might marry a Japanese girl, Sada a Pakistani girl, Bhaji an English, Rajen a Chinese, Babji a French, and Rajee a Russian. What will come of it? Your decision may hinder the arranging of Aru's marriage and other marriages thereafter. Another question: Will she as a foreign wife, be able to live with you all your life? It is an absolute truth that foreign women do not remain married with their husbands for long, and especially do not stay in India. Then, how would she adjust in our family environment? Will she be like other women in the family?

He urged me to think about all these issues. Since the brother who naively pointed out the adverse effects of my decision to marry abroad was staying with my older sister-in-law at that time, they must have conferred on what to write and emphasize in their respective prose. Their storylines were somewhat similar. My sister-in-law's letter, however, was acceptably positive. She had affirmed my decision to marry.

> We have always accepted your decisions. How could we not? Further, these days even in India boys and girls find their own companions. Pramo had told us that our mother has written a letter to you. No one knows the content of that letter. If she has written some harsh words, please do not consider it ill and answer her politely. But you have not written when you are coming. Whether you come alone or not you must return to India. Everyone, including the younger ones, remain eager for you to return. They miss you. Please do not be angry with the contents of anyone's letter. I am waiting for your answer soon.

Indian joint family milieu can be melodramatic. The elders require total obedience and loyalty. A growing young man has no freedom to explore or think for himself. Indian parents, especially mothers, smother their offspring with irrational possessiveness and commands. As I was growing up and went to college some distance from home, I became more conscious of this fact. Whenever I would go home, I would literally suffer from lack of choices because of joint family's monitoring altruism! It was not only unreal but almost depressing and suffocating to a point where I would find reasons to either postpone my trip, shorten it, or take a detour. We were expected to depend on others for everything. There was no such thing as freedom of choice; everything had to be approved. Otherwise, it would be treated as disrespect, defiance or being egocentric. Could this have been the unconscious motivation for my extended stay abroad? Others have commented that the evil of returning to one's homeland is almost always dreaded.

Controlling as they were, the Indian families, nonetheless, always hoped for their children's wellbeing even if the youngsters tried to disconnect in their personal matters. Since everyone lived together most of the time, they were a good judge of the character also, but only from their own limited perspective and their proscribed experience. As my visit was to end soon, most misunderstandings of the past had been converted into amicable conversations. There was now a positive aura as I declared to them that from there on, I shall visit India more often. In another two weeks, my research data were collected, and I was ready to fully pack my belongings.

Just when I was preparing to leave, my sister-in-law, in private, confided with me an incident that was simply mystifying. It was, she said, soon after I had moved from Canada to the United States of America for my doctorate education. "A car pulled up in front of our family home in Gyanpur, and the passengers included a young woman in her mid-twenties, holding on to a less than two-year-old boy. They were accompanied by the girl's father."

Reportedly, she asked for my mother and introduced herself as an employee of Allahabad Institute where I worked before moving to Delhi. During the afternoon, my mother held the boy and whispered to my sister-in-law.

"That boy resembled me when I was that age."

My reaction to this story was blasé. I was not only puzzled but was unable to fully resolve that bizarre tale.

That visiting woman also told my mother and assembled siblings that she and I had the same boss, Dr. JBC. After receiving my letter from Canada, he had announced in a staff meeting that I will not be returning to the Institute to accept the newly created position of Director, Extension Training Center. This news had spurred quite an excitement among my former colleagues; no doubt, they were pleased to see one of their onetime contemporaries reach this far. We had worked together in the villages of Jamunapar for two years and had become close. We were more than a family. One of our colleagues, who took that director's job, also went to Gyanpur to meet my mother. Others close to me did that subsequently as a sign of good will and to convey good wishes. Or was it a gesture to indirectly console my mother for losing a son?

***

The situation that my mother, the older brothers and two younger siblings faced while I was abroad was the shortage of resources to educate and raise youngsters still at home. Along with that the task of helping my two younger brothers to complete their master's degrees appeared problematic. Looming on the horizon, they feared, was an impending disaster, even starvation. Desperation had set in. Hence, I was the logical person who, preferably remaining single, could assist in the family expenses. Did they not consider that to be an unreasonable expectation?

What my mother faced as a single parent was not supposed to happen in a responsible, morally sound, and caring joint family. One third of the joint family property that belonged to my mother had been denied to her. During my short visit to India, I tried to focus on the positive side of everything and did not bring up the joint family's rather callous conduct. Indirectly, however, I did mention the irony of unequal sharing of joint family wealth.

Perhaps during late 1960s, and close to my arrival, a major gathering of the joint family was held in our ancestral village. Reportedly, during that meeting the goal was to foster a verbal understanding as to the disposition of homes and agricultural property. Present at this meeting were notably my uncle and his sons and my two older brothers. Of course, women folk, including my mother were not franchised to participate in this misogynist culture.

The principle underlying the partition was the Customary Hindu Law under which when a property was acquired by any active member of the joint family, it became a part and parcel of the community property over which all had a legal right. It was with this time-honored precept that the Gyanpur and Varanasi properties were partitioned. That had been our family's customary law. The Courts of India have recognized a custom as law if the custom is, "ancient or immemorial" in origin, "reasonable" in nature, and "continuous."

That precept was based on the recognized foundation for the source of law of the land, its genesis. The Indian Constitution defines "law" to include "custom or usage," and "certain." The Courts have interpreted, "ancient or immemorial" to mean that for a custom to be binding, "it must derive its force from the fact that by long usage it has obtained the force of law." A custom also "derives its validity from being reasonable at inception and its current exercise." Lastly, a "certain" custom is one that is, "reliable in its extent and mode of operation," and invariable. What was done before could be repeated again under certain circumstances, chiefly among those who show their sincere affinity for the joint family structure and assert their claim to ancestral property.

At that gathering, after the initial proposal was laid out by two members representing homes in Gyanpur and Varanasi, respectively, a real drama was brewing. So far, no questions were raised, and the younger generation was distracted by refreshments consisting of pakoras, ghughari and jalebi. Then an angry son of the oldest dead uncle asked about his share in the ancestral home. He demanded grain to be taken to a nearby city where he lived.

His uncle calmly began to explain a practical and a just point of view. Before he could finish, his son who lived in the village home elaborated what was expressed initially. "The farm produce—crops, grain, fiber, vegetables, fruits—are the product of hard work by people who live full time and toil here." That was a fair statement. Raising his voice slightly he declared, "If you want a share, you should come and live and work here. That way you would be benefiting from your own labor, and not be taking away from the rewards of labor of others." In his typical abusive response, this maverick cousin rebuked everyone using four-letter profanity, followed by a loud cry! That was the dramatic highlight of the gathering.

Then the coolheaded members, including my two oldest brothers and our uncle's three older sons discussed the same sacred principles enumerated above. Clearly, this family's ancestors had used these guidelines to ensure the continuity of their communal property and its proper equitable utilization on a long-term basis.

So, if a member claims his legal right to a joint family property, he is entitled to his share minus what it cost to upgrade it. A property appraiser can ascertain that capital gain for the benefit of the whole. Those reprobate and absent elements who would want to claim their share would not be denied their portion. They would be welcome to come and live in the ancestral home if they would share the cost of its upkeep. Those members, who live away and earn a living for their own benefit, must contribute financially for the maintenance of a jointly claimed property. By fully sharing the cost, they would not be deprived of their legal rights, but they shall not claim the fruits of others labor. If they persist in demanding their share, they might be excommunicated with a unanimous consent of the others. That would be the only way to maintain the integrity of the community property.

At the end of this gathering a plan emerged that was called ABC:

> "A" stood for constructed portions which were primarily living spaces such as the ancestral home in our village, my parent's home in Gyanpur, and a joint-family home in nearby Varanasi. Gyanpur home was callously divided. But, strangely, our joint family home in an ancestral village was left intact and presumed to belong to everyone. "B" referred to semi-constructed or potentially constructible property. "C" referred to the unconstructed real estate such as the one across from our Gyanpur home that was *de facto* occupied by my uncle's son.

Intriguingly, the ABC plan was about living or potentially livable spaces. There was no discernible discussion about the land holdings. Focusing on just the living spaces, current or future, was such a shortsighted way of resolving joint family property that it created an unprecedented opportunity for misappropriation and future animosity. Understandably, a family meeting of this kind must have been disorienting for some members who have had an emotional attachment to the authority of a traditional joint family. Some felt constrained and did not utter a word. Others simply felt sorry for themselves, oblivious to the fact that they were on the losing end of the game. Still others, notably my older brothers, felt betrayed by their cousins who they trusted. The clandestine move by our elderly cousins was a boon for them at our expense.

This was a monumental event in the history of this ill-fated joint family. Sadly, I was not informed about it. Not a word was said about this to me during my visits. What were they thinking when they decided to keep this to themselves? Did I not belong to their family? Or was it too shameful to have lost what was ours? Be that as it may, it was clear to me that they thought that since I was an occasional visitor, I did not have to know about the family impropriety. Either they were sparing me from the joint family chicanery and squabbles, or they were too embarrassed to apprise me of the deception.

On this short 1966 trip to India, it seemed that much had changed in my family's life and they were unwilling to share with me the reprehensible inner dynamics of our joint family. Externally, it was an impermeable force to deal with by the outsiders, but internally it was a bundle of conniving, jealous, greedy, mean, and self-serving entity. Like three branches of a tree symbolizing three brothers, my father being the youngest, each branch's strength depended on the number and age of their stems. The oldest branch, now dead, had only two stems that were revered by the others. They could and did claim more than their share due to the old practice of primogeniture. The middle live branch had four sturdy stems and three others who were being heftily nurtured by the surviving head. The youngest branch with only one strong and one weak stem, alongside six dependent children, was in real jeopardy.

As in the past, before leaving my homeland, I visited our ancestral village and implored at the familial temple complex for mercy from our ancestors and a plea to rescue their putrefying descendants.

Also, I travelled to the nearby shrine named after the Goddess of *Vindhyachal*. That was the holy shrine where all the family toddlers, me included, having survived the first five years of their life, were taken for an initiation ceremony—head shaving, ear piercing, and giving a formal name. I supplicated the most revered *Vindhyavasini* to bless my wife with a child. That famed Goddess has been rightly hallowed for shielding children and is venerated throughout the country as a formidable deity.

V

At the end of August 1966, I returned to my alma mater and felt satisfied about my accomplishments in India. Both goals of visiting India, that is mending fences with my primary family members, and collecting the PhD dissertation data were vigorously pursued. Pleased and feeling blessed, I brought with me completed interview protocols from ninety respondents.

The entire package of completed questionnaires was submitted to several members of the faculty for scrutiny, especially those who were familiar with my research design. They were satisfied and gave me a go-ahead with its analysis. To do that, I had to enroll in Graduate Research courses. That enabled me to use the library, the computer center, and obtain the academic guidance from my mentors. Now the challenge was to analyze the data using specific computer programs, followed by interpretations of data in a lucid way.

My dissertation research was about civic attitudes and social change in India. The data brought from India was suitable for carrying out a threefold analysis: first, to delineate clusters of attitudes toward modernization and social change; second, to describe system-types based on the interaction between attitude clusters, and finally, to develop typologies of the modernizing elite.

The genesis of this subject can be traced to a survey of social science literature that identified certain components of a society that gave the structure of governance its unique distinction. These were called political objects--a community, the regime, and the authorities. These three were utilized for studying not only the developmental policies but an attempt was made to ascertain the nature of orientation toward these objects.

The analysis of orientation toward these three objects consisted of a two-step paradigm, linking the basic personality needs with the individual predispositions, and then linking predispositions with specific attitudes toward the objects. The central linkage mechanism was called the Latent Attitude Structure or LAS. The LAS was measured with the help of a Dogmatism Scale. This paradigm helped in hypothesizing about several relationships between attitudes and the governing objects. This dissertation research was both substantive as well as methodological.

The entire data was analyzed principally by means of a technique known as factor analysis, one of the statistical devices I had learned in Canada. At my United States alma-mater, however, I met an eminent English methodologist who guided me toward specific data analysis strategies. Principally, it was a heuristic device that caused reduction of data to a few essential categories of relationships. On the one hand, factor analysis served to explore new kinds of relationships, and on the other, it was useful for testing hypotheses. Of many kinds of factor analysis, two suitable variations ("R" and "Q" methods) were chosen. The "R" method referred to intercorrelations between attitudinal statements resulting in unique configurations, and the "Q" method (obverse of "R") involved correlations between persons yielding clusters of personality profiles.

Along with the data analysis, though I had finished all my course requirements, I continued to audit courses, particularly in my primary field of comparative studies. But most of the time, I was occupied with the analysis and interpretation, i.e., transferring data to IBM punch cards and submitting those to the Computer Center for specified analysis. During this phase, as mentioned above, I had to be officially enrolled to use the various campus facilities such as the university computer, a study carrel in the library, checking out books, and requesting inter-university library loans.

At the end of that academic year, I must have had a ton of computer printout sheets piled sixty to seventy inches high on the floor of my apartment. It was a productive year. At last, I could see a light at the end of the tunnel! Also, 1967 was a singularly distinctive year—my wife gave birth to a beautiful girl. We celebrated her arrival and named her after Goddess *Vindhyavasini*. That holy ground was near a village where I was born. I wrote to my mother to send my younger brother to pay homage to the Goddess.

There comes a point when a researcher knows that he has fully exploited the data at hand. When I was satisfied with the length and breadth of data analysis, I began to interpret and describe the results. All through these steps of data analysis and writing, I had weekly meetings with my primary dissertation adviser. Although he was an expert in analyzing voting patterns, dissimilar to what I was delving into, he made unprecedented effort to keep up with my pace. He gave my project full attention despite his hectic schedule, having to allocate his time to other students. His keen analytical mind and his specialized research skills helped me immensely. In many ways we were like-minded researchers. Later, the adviser commented that mine was the first empirically oriented PhD dissertation ever produced in that department.

Most colleges and universities launch their recruitment for new faculty in earnest beginning the winter semester. During that semester of 1967, a faculty adviser, who was also the placement director for the department, had compiled a folder of new job openings from throughout the country. Essentially, these were one-page job descriptions. All graduating students looking for a job would go to his office and glance through the folder in his presence. I found just a handful of descriptions that suited me. Two stood out: Hastings College in Nebraska, and a new campus of California State University system. When I was writing down the address of the latter, the placement director stated, "That is for our own boys!" Earlier in our conversation my own adviser had commented that I should aim for a job at a nationally recognized university, and not go back to the university in Louisiana. By that I understood that I was now overqualified to apply for a Black college.

Of all the universities I had applied for a job, I received definite offers from Nebraska, California, and Louisiana. The latter was out of the question because I could not get any favorable recommendation letters to join that college. The dean from Hastings College called and wanted me to come to his campus for an interview. I had talked to him extensively two or three times. At one point, I alerted him to the fact that I was married to an American. The dean replied, "We like Americans too!" We both understood what was meant by that statement, i.e., alluding to the culture of racism. It was mutually agreed to set a date for an interview soon.

The following day the personnel secretary of California State University rang up and asked if I could meet their president on a certain date across the old Kansas City Airport in the lobby of a Holiday Inn. So, I met the president of that institution, and the interview went well. As soon as he returned to his campus, the vice president of that institution called to offer me an assistant professor's job. I informed him that I needed to think about it, and to talk to my professors. The following day, I consulted my campus employer who explained to me the hierarchy of institutions of higher education in California. He recommended that I should accept the offer but did not have to stay there. I talked to two other professors who agreed to write letters in my behalf. When the next call came from California, I informed the vice president that I had a year's teaching experience at a university in Louisiana. He understood my position and upped my salary range.

Now the phase had arrived when I could assemble and finalize all the interpretations of my dissertation data in a coherent way, chapter by chapter. That was followed by writing the introductory chapter and a conclusion. The advantage was that I had already compiled an extensive bibliographic material and there was not a single piece of related literature on the topic that had escaped me. As I would be writing a chapter, something would necessitate that I do further analysis, just to satisfy my curiosity, or confirm the results. I had become a compulsive researcher, not to leave any stone unturned! All through this hectic period, I had just one notable confrontation with my primary faculty adviser. He seemed to be overwhelmed with his workload and hinted that I needed to slow down. I retorted rather bluntly that I wanted to leave the town at the end of that academic year. Finally, I think he understood the urgency especially because of a job waiting for me in California.

At the end of the academic year, I had completed the final draft of my PhD dissertation. After it was approved by my adviser, the dissertation was typed and readied for duplication. There were no computer word processors in those days. The Graduate office recommended an approved professional typist who completed the task on her electric typewriter. All pages had to be flawless; no corrections were allowed. Five copies of my four-hundred-page dissertation, weighing six pounds each, had to be submitted to the Graduate School office. It cost a thousand dollars which I borrowed from the National Science Foundation funds that were set aside for such a purpose.

By the latter half of Spring term of 1968, all my degree requisites were completed, and the dissertation had reached its final draft. The problem was that valuable time had slipped by. Because it was the end of the academic year, my committee members were either under a deadline to complete their grading or were planning for the summer. Nevertheless, my adviser promised to schedule a committee meeting early next semester. "At this stage, it was all a formality," he told me. Nonetheless, neither he nor I wanted to postpone a meeting with the dissertation committee. The urgency of orally presenting my research findings to the committee was on my mind while we drove to California.

Amidst all these uncertainties, our newly acquired Impala Station wagon was finally packed with important luggage; five duplicated copies of my PhD dissertation, picnic food for the rest stops, and a crib in the back seat for a one-year-old Vindhya. Our first stop was in Nevada,

Missouri, about one-hundred miles southwest to meet my wife's parents. From there we drove to Enid, Oklahoma, to meet and stay overnight with the parents of a dear friend who was also working on his doctorate degree. His father owned the local newspaper. They were gracious hosts. Sometimes non-relatives can be the most hospitable of all.

From Oklahoma we travelled westward, stopping every two to three hours because our toddler did not like to be cooped up in the car. Eventually, we reached California in five days, traveling some fifteen-hundred miles.

When we were driving down the interstate, it was a hot afternoon, and we could see fires up and down the sides of the road. We looked at each other and wondered where we were headed. What kind of a place was this? Even with the inferno all around we were eager to reach our destination.

As expected, within four days of our arrival in California, I flew back to campus and was a guest of the professor who had rented the same apartment that we had lived in for three years. My oral examination was scheduled for the following Friday. Since my host did not have a car, we walked a mile to the campus, hot, sweaty, coughing, and puffing.

I was a little nervous to enter the committee room on that Friday, and to face the distinguished faculty members. I was anxious about the kinds of questions they might ask. What if they did not approve of my dissertation research? Once the first question was raised about my methodology, I felt at ease. I reckon, I knew more about that theme than the rest of them, except of course my saintly adviser. Although the questions were largely on the dissertation, they wanted to know about my intellectual growth. More than simply asking about the methodology pertaining to my research and the general findings, the committee was principally directing my attention to the pedagogical matters in a broad sense. Obviously, they wanted to ascertain my *weltanschauung*.

I began by declaring that my upbringing was first and foremost in the space of being in the moment and paying attention to the present, i.e., looking at a situation seriously and not dreaming. As I grew up in an upper caste family of landlords, I understood that my elders were preparing me to be mindful of the grandeur of nature and society. In technical terms, they referred to a state of consciousness in which the difference between me and others, who were of lesser economic class, should inevitably fade. It felt like transcendence from dichotomy to oneness was to be my goal in life. I was taught that everything was a part of and made of one non-dual consciousness.

Was that upbringing aimed at "ontological" contentment? Often, the question arises, "If it is all one thing, why don't we experience it that way?" While young, this was confusing to us. How could the concept of oneness be equal to the appearance of sameness?

"Things can appear different without being separate," we were taught. The objects, animals, plants, and people in the world are all different in their appearance and functioning. But they are all connected at their source—they come from the same cradle. When our experience of reality becomes more subtle, we discover that everything is merely different expressions of one field of non-dual being. In the teachings of Vedanta, the truth about non-dual consciousness, or oneness of being, has often been thought of as something hidden, and difficult to experience. Upon further study, however, it would appear quite ordinary and accessible in every moment. Non-dual consciousness is the natural state. Of course, a dramatic experience of oneness is a rare event, but still it exists. We are all the same at various stages in life. Truth is one.

In empirical social sciences, we replicate our research findings, and our hypotheses have a chance of discerning the same truth universally. In essence, truth about equality of all living beings can be ascertained universally.

I felt that I communicated well with the committee. Indeed, I had given serious thought to the implications of the major findings of my research, i.e., modernizing and socially changing societies from the ashes of foreign colonization, and their oppressive rule's long-term impact on our psyche. The challenge was to bring them at par with the rest of the modern world. It had great potential especially because after independence a sense of confidence and a desire for equality had created a modern set of institutions. By this time, I was effortlessly conversational. I blurted out my responses relentlessly unaware that I was being judged.

Our colloquy lasted for close to an hour. At the end, I heard an "applause!" Everyone got up, and as they left the room, they shook my hand and congratulated me. This was a clear indication that I was acceptable to them as a scholar, and that I shall be granted a doctorate degree. My adviser had them sign the last page of my dissertation which was forwarded to the Graduate office for registration and binding.

Outside the committee room my admirable adviser urged me to attend the department's picnic that evening. There, I mingled with everyone, finding the fellow graduate students cold with jealousy. Not only that I was now a PhD degree recipient but had a tenure track teaching job at a state university in California. What more could one ask? Uneasy in their company, I moved over to where the professors were gathered. There, what was touching was the way my adviser introduced me. I was affably bowled over. He fought tears and with a lump in his throat uttered. "Only I know what this scholar (pointing to me) has accomplished today. Where he was when he came to me four years ago and where he is today." That was a heartwarming moment. I choked with emotions and tears rolled down my cheeks as it has in composing this paragraph. Indeed, between 1964 and 1968, I had completed a master's degree, taught for a year at a university in New Orleans, and was now granted a Doctor of Philosophy degree.

An American novelist of *The Great Gatsby* fame, Francis Scott Fitzgerald, once remarked that there were no second acts. He could not have known about the new genre of gritty foreign students who proved that there could be a flaming real American story in the second act.

When I returned to California, I was relaxed and gratified for having achieved my primary goal in life. The following Monday when I arrived on campus, I had a letter from my alma mater declaring that I had, "Completed all the requirements for a PhD degree." I delivered that to the chair of the social sciences division. Promptly, he walked it over to the vice president's office and my personnel file was updated. Instantly, that letter of certification restored my rank and salary to Assistant Professor fourth level. I was now a legitimate scholar; holding a PhD degree and was an employee of an institution of higher learning. It was an overwhelming experience that took longer to soak in and absorb.

Ostensibly, I had come a long way. With a PhD degree and a tenure track teaching job, I was set in life for now, though not in the country I would have preferred to settle down. But we do not have control over our destiny. Divine providence was in control. It was my fortune, at least for now, to perch at a major American university, excel in being a scholar and a teacher. It is not that I would not encounter professional and personal obstacles, but they would likely be akin to brush fires.

VI

All through the sixties, intense social upheaval was churning American society—many cities were set on fire due to racial riots. Of those, the Watts riot in Southern California in 1968, where we were to live, was noticeably alarming. Even before we left the Midwest, people were warning us about going to California. At a physician's office prior to our departure, I was asked, "Do you know where you are going? It showed how edgy everyone was because a feeling of vulnerability in America was pervasive.

The term Watts's riot refers to a large-scale race war which lasted six days in the southern part of Los Angeles, California. By the time the riot subsided, thirty-four people had been killed, a thousand injured, and close to four-thousand arrested. It would stand as the worst uprising in Los Angeles history until it was eclipsed by another in 1992.

The Watts riot began when a California highway patrol motorcycle officer pulled over a Black driver. He was suspected of intoxication because of his erratic driving; he failed the sobriety test. Not being able to walk in a straight line while holding his nose, he was immediately arrested. The officer refused to let the driver's brother take away the car home and radioed for it to be impounded. As events escalated, a crowd of onlookers steadily grew from a handful to hundreds. The mob became violent, throwing rocks and sticks while shouting at the police officers. A struggle ensued resulting in the arrest of the driver, his brother, and their mother.

Before our arrival in the area, there had been a gradual buildup of racial tension. Violence not only erupted periodically in different parts of Los Angeles, but racial slurs were freely exchanged in shopping malls and workplaces. As the ferocity was displayed sporadically across the city, businesses suffered from looting, fighting, and vandalism that seriously threatened the security of the metropolis. Some accomplices chose to intensify the level of violence by starting physical fights with police, blocking firemen of the Los Angeles fire department from their safety duties, or even beating the passing White motorists. Others broke into stores, hauling whatever they could, and setting the store on fire. Casually, the inciters wandered the streets encouraging the potential rioters, and giving the police a difficult time.

Reportedly, the Los Angeles Police Department chief knowingly fueled the radicalized tension that already threatened to combust by publicly labeling those involved in the riots as, "monkeys in the zoo." Overall, the damage amounted to forty million dollars and almost one-thousand buildings were destroyed. Most of the physical destruction was confined to White and Asian-owned businesses that were said to have caused resentment in the Black neighborhood because they were unfairly treated. Private homes were not attacked, although some caught fire due to their proximity to burning structures.

With destructive events in the United States galloping faster and faster, 1968 quickly developed into a year of rage. Across America emotions ran high. Tensions peaked when two notable leaders who had brought the promise of hope to a generation were assassinated. A harsh blow came to the Civil Rights movement when Martin Luther King, Jr., was assassinated on April 4, 1968, followed by the assassination of one of the anti-war movement's hopefuls. That person was none other than Robert F. Kennedy who in the early morning of June 5, 1968, was shot point blank in a hotel. Kennedy died twenty-six hours later. I was being warned about this unfolding doomsday scenario in California because it could jeopardize the safety of every colored man.

Another event soon followed. The 1968 Democratic national

convention was to commence at the International Amphitheatre in Chicago, Illinois. The purpose of that convention was for the election of a suitable nominee to run as the Democratic party's choice for the post of President of the United States of America. Chicago's mayor, Richard J. Daley, intended to showcase his city's achievements to national Democrats and the news media. Instead, the proceedings garnered media attention and notoriety because of the large number of demonstrators and the use of force by the Chicago police during what was supposed to be, as branded by Yippee activist organizers, "A Festival of Life." The rioting, which then took place between demonstrators and the Chicago police department and the Illinois national guard, was well publicized in the mass media. Almost all of those present experienced firsthand what the protestors at Chicago also suffered. Well-known newsmen of the day, Mike Wallace and Dan Rather, were both roughed up by the Chicago police inside the convention hall.

One person who did not attend the convention was the incumbent President Lyndon B. Johnson, who several months earlier had announced that he would neither seek nor accept the nomination for the presidency.

After the assassination of President John F. Kennedy, the position of President fell to then Vice President Johnson. Unfortunately, he inherited the baggage of the Vietnam War. Mr. Johnson, who was less interested in foreign affairs than his forerunner, found the war an annoyance. Instead, he hoped to establish America's sense of purpose on the national stage and not in the international arena. He did this by pushing for the 1964 Civil Rights Act, originally a proposal of Kennedy, and followed it up with the implementation of 1965 Voting Rights Act. Together these two pieces of legislation became the most significant civil rights laws since the Thirteenth Amendment to the U.S. Constitution.

Unfortunately, the fact that the Korean War had ended in a stalemate, not a victory for America, President Johnson felt that if he did not support the Vietnam War the opposition would label him soft on communism. Therefore, he used the 1964 Gulf of Tonkin resolution as a reason to escalate the conflict. Thus, he prolonged America's unpopular war that caused havoc. More than fifty-eight thousand Americans died, and more than three million Vietnamese perished. It would forever stain America as well as Vietnam. Thereafter, the people at home began to oppose the war. Events of this nature were constantly evolving and that alone afforded me with rich current data for my international relations classes that I would teach.

The Vietnam War that was broadcast nightly on the Six O'clock news, though it benefited the knowledge gatherers like me, tended to create a heavy burden on people's psyche. Even America's most reliable journalist, Walter Cronkite, had said that the war would end in a stalemate. That not only alarmed but depressed the president who felt that Cronkite's comment would steer public opinion even further away from prolonging the war in Vietnam. The statement of Cronkite was probably another contributing factor in President Johnson's choice for not seeking a second term.

There were other reasons for his decision. He was not only ill but physically and psychologically exhausted. Also, he had lost control of the political process. Only thirty-five percent of American voters approved President Johnson's policies. Even though he could have won the Democratic nomination through backroom politics, yet it would have split the organization. Public opinion had shown that he was popular with neither the right nor the left wing of his party. He realized, therefore, that the wisest course of action for him was not to run.

***

Prior to our arrival in California, we were in constant touch with a faculty wife who was on their welcoming committee. A motel room was reserved for us when we arrived in town. After we checked into it and rested for a while, we began to feel hungry. By chance we chose a Mexican café for dinner that evening and decided to try their "burritos"—love at first bite! Coming from mid-America, this town looked and felt like an exotic place.

After two days of confinement in that oppressive motel room, we moved into a rental home closer to campus in the northern part of town. When the neighbors saw our license plate, they became nostalgic and welcomed us to their neighborhood. They themselves had come from the mid-Western states during the 1940s, following World War II.

The next day, I went to campus and met my boss, an affable scholar. His administrative secretary was also very cordial. I was properly received, briefed, and taken to my office in the Administration building where all incoming faculty were housed.

Before my colleagues and I joined the division of social sciences, there were only a limited number of faculties on board. One in my area of specialty was responsible for scheduling courses for all new faculty. However, major decisions for the departments were made by the head of the social sciences division. Later, I discovered that he too had to consult with the president and the vice president on all faculty related matters. Truly, it was a centralized administration then.

During the faculty orientation gathering, the first official day of the academic year 1968-69, I met all newly hired professors, a rather large contingency, which had joined the campus. A total of four new instructors, including myself, were added to my department alone. During our briefing there was a comprehensive exposure to the campus in terms of its mission, the educational philosophy, and support facilities.

The campus was buzzing with people. Soon the task of classroom instruction would begin. I was assigned three courses that amounted to twelve units of instruction for the fall term. The enrollment in classes was small, this being a new campus that had opened its doors only three years back with five-hundred students. The enrollment by the fall of 1968 had tripled to about fifteen hundred. Students appeared eager to learn and were not hesitant to ask questions during the class period. The faculty was expected to offer seminars akin to Socratic dialogs. Straight lectures which we were accustomed to in our student days were frowned upon and discouraged.

In general, the predominantly White faculty seemed very friendly despite their inherently myopic, culturally parochial, and paranoiac leanings. They seemed alien to their non-White colleagues. Whatever their cultural and personal biases, outwardly they appeared accepting. Someone who later became a close friend admitted that they were raised to suspect all non-White people. As a quirk from the days of slavery, the colored human beings were deemed to be inferior and not equal to White or grey, or pink Europeans. The verdict from the top college administrators, notably the president, the academic vice president, and few others was vague. No doubt they had instructions from the Chancellor's office of the State University system to muster a diverse faculty because of a vastly assorted population in the state. A trend toward adopting a policy of inclusiveness was a gambit because of a large population of African Americans, Asians, and Hispanics in the service area.

The university campus which I had joined was touted not only as, the "Harvard of the Desert," and written up in *Harper's Magazine* in 1967, but was a unique instructional campus that had embarked on a strong liberal arts curriculum. It was fashioned after the pedagogy developed at the University of Chicago. To begin with, there would be no inter-collegiate sports. That point of reference attracted most of the pioneering faculty including myself. For a Baccalaureate degree the college required ninety units of general education courses, two foreign languages, and a comprehensive examination before awarding a BA degree. Of all other comparable institutions in Southern California, this was a very demanding program. As time went by and students began to by-pass our institution, we became alarmed and started to attenuate our curricula. It became obvious that we lacked an appropriate fit of curricula for this depressed and working-class region.

As a civically conservative son of a Czech immigrant, the founder-president was a person who had bought into and was trying to sell a liberal arts package that was not in sync with the constituency, and the regional inland culture of Southern California. As changes had to be made for reasons of institutional survival, he had to often look the other way. He was a unique person with impressive social skills. As a child of White immigrant parents, in many respects, his life and success resembled that of the privileged upper class educated citizens.

This college's chief executive officer was three years of age when his parents migrated to Chicago from Croatia. After completing his PhD degree from the University of Chicago he found his first teaching job at Chico State college, also a part of State University system. When our new campus was chartered under the California Master Plan for Higher Education, the Chancellor of the CSU system, another Croatian American, appointed our president to this post. He in turn brought with him a team consisting of two Chico State professors, also Chicago graduates.

They rented a large house in the downtown area of the city as the campus headquarters. That multistoried house served as the planning office for the proposed institution. With the support of the local business community and major real estate developers, one-hundred acres of land at the rate of one dollar per acre was acquired in the northern part of the city. This land had been an abandoned vineyard. State and Federal funds were made available for constructing campus buildings.

In the wake of Russian Sputnik having been fired into space, the supremacy of Russian scientific achievement was seriously overshadowing the image of the United States as a superpower. Therefore, Federal funds were readily available to construct the first two science buildings on campus. The race for enhanced science education was on in full measure. Also, numerous other offices, a temporary library and other facilities sprung up before the influx of new faculty, including me, in the fall of 1968.

My office was in one corner of the sprawling, single-story administration building. In private conversations my colleagues would assert how the president administered that campus as if it were his personal plantation! Indeed, during afternoons, just to relax, he would walk around without his jacket, and you could predict that he would pass by your office and exchange greetings. Truly he was a shrewd chap who understood how to administer certain difficult rules without giving the impression that it was indeed not his decision. He had planted his honchos in every nook and cranny of the campus. Wanting to feel empowered; few of his subordinates, invariably, turned out to be the evil guys.

During the original planning of the campus, all architectural and construction decisions had to be approved by the Chancellor's office. In that office there was a bureaucrat who was renowned by his rivals as the obstructionist. As a clever administrative move, our president hired him as his vice president for campus planning. It so happened that the new administrator was a graduate of my own university. Thus, he was a fellow alumnus, and I had a strong pillar to rely on.

Being a new campus, with minimum faculty and fewer students, it did not appear as a noteworthy institution of higher learning. In those days, the job applicants were not asked to come to campus for interviews. Instead, the president, and later vice presidents and even the deans, would travel around the country to interview prospective candidates.

***

The three assigned courses that I taught in the fall of 1968 term comprised a third of my annual teaching load. Each class met three times per week, but students earned five units per class—three hours for attending lectures and two hours for completing assignments, which included spending research time in the library. Preparing for teaching three new courses was a very hectic schedule for me. However, the next time it was easier to prepare for the same courses. In addition to lecture preparation on a weekly basis, faculty were expected to be professionally active, i.e., remaining effective in doing research, participating in conferences, publishing, and engaging in service-area community activities.

The class enrollments were small, sometimes as low as five. Much was expected of students; indeed, they had to complete their assignments as well as participate in class discussions. To reiterate, the classes were not straight lecture sessions. The institutional pedagogy was to fully encourage student participation. My own style was to lecture for ten to fifteen minutes at the outset to set the stage for focused discussions. My syllabi for the courses were comprehensive and, therefore, it was easy for students to follow a daily schedule of lessons. Textbooks were required for students along with library reserve items for additional reading.

In addition to classroom hours, we had to schedule office hours for students so they could visit and get help with lessons. These visits were intense during a student's senior year when they had to plan for their future—planning to pursue further education or applying for a job. There were many students who grew up without parents and lacked supportive guardians. They would try to use us as sounding boards. I had one such student who came to us at age eighteen after completing high school. He was raised by his German aunt. I guided him through the four years of his college education and got him placed as an intern in the office of a local state legislature. Later, largely because of his internship experience, and developing negotiation skills, he was elected to the California state legislature. In our scholarly endeavors there were many such magical moments when we succeeded in helping place students on their choice of career path—be that internship, law school, or graduate school.

Supplementary to our scholarly activities, for which we spent up to a decade in graduate school, we had two other discrete efforts to engage in and make our academic life complete. In graduate school we had no training in either committee work, or community involvement. Yet these became the realm of getting to know the university service area—truly an on-the-job training. They were, however, arbitrary areas for determining the effectiveness of faculty.

Each campus was administered using a committee system, and every faculty was expected to participate in those. There were committees at the department, college, and university levels. In addition, there was a statewide faculty senate as well. Participation was not automatic, however. Regular elections were held to fill the vacancies. Most significant was my election to one of two faculty senate positions from my campus to the statewide faculty senate. I served in that senate for three, three-year terms. At the state level we were involved in deliberations on issues related to curriculum development, degree requirements, and general policies in academic administration. As a member of the statewide faculty senate, it was required that I attend the campus faculty senate meetings each month. Although the college president and the academic vice president regularly attended the monthly faculty senate meetings, they could not vote. Nevertheless, the committee recommendations were forwarded to them for final approval, and implementation.

A third area of faculty involvement was euphemistically called, "town and gown" activities. It could simply be to speak at an event. Or bringing a dignitary, especially a national leader, or inviting a travelling scholar from abroad. I too volunteered to speak to various civic groups locally.

My involvement in launching a high school Model United Nations program on campus was noteworthy. An employee of the city's Mayoral Commission on Tourism had an idea which she came to share with the university administration. She wanted an instructor who taught international relations to help organize a Model United Nations program using the local high school students. A large room was set aside for this event at the newly built city shopping mall. For this, I was sought out by the dean of social and behavioral sciences. To institute that project, I had to train my students to take up a joint project of conducting a mock session of the United Nations tapping the local high school students. A simulation of the Model United Nations required actual participation in a similar exercise at a higher level by my own students.

Hence, in 1974, I took a group of my students to New York City to participate in the National Model United Nations. It was a heady stuff. Having been exposed to the workings of the United Nations inside the U.N. headquarters itself my students realized the immensity of the role the actual United Nations ambassadors played after the Second World War.

With an acquired experience of how the actual United Nations worked, they were expected to facilitate the staging of a high school Model U.N. when they returned to campus.

New York trips ended in 1976, primarily because of high cost of travel, and exorbitant hotel expenses. Instead, the president of the university advised me to take our students to Model United Nations of the Far West (MUNFW), that was held at university campuses on the west coast. The funds for that project were made available through the student contingency fee. My travel expenses came from the college of social and behavioral sciences. That went on until 1985, when the quality of the western Model U.N. deteriorated to an intolerable extent. Students began to treat this outing as a partying occasion. There was no redeeming quality to it. Their drunken episodes became dangerous for all. Various faculty advisors including myself had lost interest and quit attending. Even my students did not want to go back to MUNFW. Then, they themselves came up with the idea of resuming our participation at the national Model United Nations in New York City, and we resumed that original plan in 1987. I continued that curricular activity until my retirement in 1998. The program was institutionalized to a permanent level, and it endured after my retirement.

***

In the mid-1960s, college students around the world became increasingly concerned about social issues such as war, poverty, hunger, prejudice, and declining quality of life. They found many causes of their liking such as anti-poverty, anti-war, and anti-censorship to rally behind. American students, in particular, discovered links between the university and the institutional apparatus supporting the United States' involvement in the Vietnam War. To be precise, the Tet Offensive of 1968 proved to be the turning point of the Vietnam War. President Johnson pointlessly tried to convince the American people that the war was being won and that administration policies were succeeding. Most American students were particularly vocal about the Vietnam War, which dragged on until 1975.

Young people on college campuses were also deeply disturbed about the lack of equality in the "land of the free," and while expressing their disgust they pushed for change. They sought to end the consensus culture that created calm after the storm following the last World War. They yearned to eliminate racial discrimination and free the oppressed from the authoritarian rule of the establishment.

These sentiments required conversion into actions that could create specific movements for social change regarding the Civil Rights movement, the Vietnam War, the women's rights, the gay rights, and goals for a reversal of the environmental degradation.

We saw the sixties as a time of radical thinkers and felt a desperate need for change. But there was no coherent crusade with a defined leadership that could articulate a national focus on resolute public policies. American political system needed a new generation of leaders who could galvanize the youth movement and consign it to a national agenda.

As part of inviting national leaders to campus, a committee at the university level, headed by a progressive vice president for academic administration, encouraged a colleague and myself to invite a popular upcoming younger senator from the state of Delaware. He was touted as the future president of the country. We invited him to visit our campus and speak on the topic of the evolving role of youth in American democracy.

The senator's calendar enabled him to visit our campus on a Wednesday in February 1975. I was designated to receive him at Ontario International Airport. I parked a rented Cadillac on the curve outside the arrival gate and went inside the terminal and saw the senator and his younger brother walking toward me. We shook hands and walked outside where the car was parked. While his brother sat on the rear seat of the car, the senator occupied the passenger seat. We carried on a general conversation about this area of California, and before long we were on campus. I remember two specific points about our conversation while I drove. First, the senator kept his brother engaged in our conversation. Second, not once did the senator ask me about my nationality, who I was, what were my subjects, and how long have I been in this country. He treated me as if we knew each other, and indeed I was who I was! I was not a foreigner but an American. When I arrived on campus, I parked the car in the visitor's lot and took a short walk to the administration building where the university president was waiting for us. The senator thanked me for the ride and shook my hands. I was just in time to teach a regularly scheduled class. While the senator was escorted to a luncheon meeting by the president along with a group of senior professors, I taught a seminar class and then heard the guest's presentation in the auditorium.

The senator began his talk with an outline of the alternative ideals of interest to younger audience. "The counterculture lifestyle on college campuses," he affirmed, "has integrated many of the noble archetypes, including peace, love, harmony, music, and mysticism. I am a little mystified [audience laughter] that meditation, yoga, and psychedelic drugs were often embraced as routes to expanding one's consciousness. The peace sign has become a major symbol of the counterculture of the 1960s. But these are difficult for the mainstream to comprehend," he warned his audience.

Our distinguished guest emphasized that one cannot understand the student awakening pertaining to the modern-day challenges without understanding that it happened three weeks after Martin Luther King Jr. was assassinated. He asked the students to think first about the survival and welfare of our country at a critical juncture such as this. To paraphrase, he asked the students to figure out ways to rebuild America—expand its social life, rejuvenate its institutions, and strive to bring everyone under one umbrella. Surely that might create a new all-encompassing America. Young people today should, he implored, get involved in the political process, and replace the old establishment with a new one. Those changes should have their stamp on it. Therefore, it is a choice between easy career and a public service career to modernize the country we all love, he concluded.

The other notable guests whom I was instrumental in bringing to campus during a ten-year period were the United Nations ambassadors of Australia, Haiti, and Thailand. In addition, I welcomed Senator

Jerry Pettis who represented this area in the United States' Senate. A professor from the University of Zimbabwe visiting Chicago accepted my invitation to visit us and give a public talk sponsored by the dean of international students. The visitor was my guest for a day.

Concisely, a faculty member's promotion, retention, and tenure in the state university system depended on his or her scores pertaining to teaching, professional development, and community service. In my case, I was diligent in preparing courses and developing sound rapport with students, fellow faculty, and staff. As was mentioned above, students also evaluated their teachers by anonymously completing a survey known as the Student Evaluation of Teacher Effectiveness (SETE). SETE scores became a part of our personnel folder. Also, our peers visited our classes periodically and submitted reports on what they observed during a class. All of these became part of a faculty's personnel folder.

Teaching at the university level was a stressful and labor-intensive job. For a duration of about ten months, it was a twenty-four-seven effort. The hours were long because after dinner in the evening we had to prepare, revise, and revamp our lecture plans for the following day. Invariably, we waited for the end of the term for a break. For such an arduous task that it was, it became necessary to seek release at the end of each of the three terms. Luckily, someone on the faculty, preferably a well to do senior faculty who had a sprawling home up on a hill, would invite everyone for a night of partying—relaxing, bonding, camaraderie, and ingenious ways of unwinding. Menfolk were simply glad to get their hands on a bottle of cold beer, never failing to find more as the evening progressed. Women, especially the younger ones, had a different idea; they were brainier, craftier, and slicker. They wanted the real spirit to soak in like a lady, not guzzle like their crude men—something that would work instantly but surely, without being suspected. They also had to drive their drunken men home safely at the end of the party without detection. Surreptitiously, therefore, they had set up an undisclosed wardrobe in the house where bottles of Brandy, Cognac, Gin, Rum, Tequila, Vodka, and Whisky were at their disposal. Vodka and Tequila were the prime choice.

One by one, each willing female guest would be escorted toward the secret area where they would go in and close the door. They would then find a glass with their name to pour the drink of their choice, and then they would open their purse, take out their fresh tampon, soak that in their drink and insert it in their vagina. Depending on their soaking potency, they may return for recharging. When you put a vodka-soaked tampon up your vagina rather than ingesting it orally, the alcohol goes into your bloodstream faster; hence, you will not know how sloshed you wanted to get. But a tampon can only soak up one shot of alcohol, which is not going to get you plastered.

Obviously, people who work hard also play hard. But diligence was never sacrificed. Faculty were expected to enhance and sustain their professional development throughout their teaching career. Included in this category were publications and presentations of research papers at conferences. There was a lot of pressure on their time and energy. My first attendance at a conference was in the Ozarks where in 1969 my former professors were assembled to share their research undertakings. I was invited to deliver a paper on, "Student Political Orientations," based on data that I had collected from my classes. The paper was well received, and I was awarded a plaque for the "Best Paper," along with a letter of appreciation. I am sure it counted, among other things, toward my retention as an assistant professor during the 1969-70 academic year. Thereafter, I attended up to three conferences annually at regional, national as well as international levels. During my active professional life, I participated in the conferences organized by various social science disciplines at local, national, and international levels in Munich, Berlin, Germany; Moscow, U.S.S.R.; Seoul, South Korea; Durban, South Africa; Quebec City, Canada; and Fukuoka, Japan. I also participated in the International Buddhist conferences held in Hamburg, Germany; Tokyo and Kyoto, Japan; and Bologna, Italy.

I had numerous research articles that were published in journals and as chapters in books. Noteworthy topics were: "Comparative Leadership in France and Italy," "Political Awareness and Learning Environments," and "Ipsative Profiles of an Indian Elite." In addition, during my teaching career I published six major books.

Ostensibly, attending conferences and publications became an important component of my career and these accomplishments were largely responsible for my timely retention during the four-year probationary period as an assistant professor, promotion to associate professor, and at the end of 1974-75 academic year to a full professor with tenure.

My colleagues who joined the faculty with me in 1968 were outgoing and trained in the broader field from land-grant universities of the Midwest. We supplemented each other but unfortunately, they moved back. Those who came afterward brought with them a different kind of scholarship. The newcomers were trained in persuasive theories with a conservative bent compared to others who, out of necessity, accepted the discipline's diversity. It was amazing how the dogmatic resolve of certain faculty hijacked the earlier calmness and camaraderie. The congenial atmosphere of the 1960's was thus transmuted into the linearity of the 1980's. It was their way or the highway! Gradually, students were also split and followed professors who spoke their partisan language. This trend crept into their lectures and counseling of students. Thus, mentoring tended to distort learning. Not only it took on the ambience of an undeviating trend in education, but the classroom discussions, likewise, lacked the aura of academic freedom. Socratic mode of instruction was transformed into partisan propaganda.

Being from the older school of thought, I continued teaching introductory courses, and I prolonged the use of my 1960's inclusive syllabi, giving equal emphasis to all existing theories, methodologies, and emerging orientations of the discipline.

The prior trend in scholarship was partly created by universities that were governed by the Morrill Act of 1862. During the earlier push for higher education reforms, the Federal government funded these so-called land-grant colleges to change the emphasis of education from classical literature to research. Morrill Act's intention was to utilize knowledge for discovery that would improve people's quality of life. Many institutions of higher learning did not choose to switch over to new pedagogy; hence, the fissure we encountered was at a level of doctrine that largely became a function of who dictated the reins, especially at a curriculum level.

It was sad that where once they had giants of intellect, sensibility, and creativity on California campuses, by the late 1980's we saw the purveyors of spectacle, imprudence, and debasement. When teachers and taught partied on the weekend with a keg of Miller High-Life, selectively engaging in proscribed social activities, where were the moral boundaries? What happened to the finer values, decency, and high culture? Where was the modicum of fidelity, and survival of the human species poised for greatness? These hedonistic indulgences in the name of fostering student-faculty rapport were draining the academe of its true purpose. Ironically, reference here is not made to the left-wing radical hippies, but to the consummate, and awed alt-right White Americans!

Even faculty recruitment and curriculum development were drastically tainted to suit the ideological bent of the ultra-scholars. It was uncanny how they would descend on a department meeting, predictably orchestrating their remarks, and voting in unison. Some who were marginal also voted for the majority for fear of being incriminated or worse, ridiculed by them.

Things were bound to vary somewhat when a new academic vice president and dean of school of social and behavioral sciences came on board. I too was elected as an acting chair and my task was to recruit a department chair from outside. The plan was to recruit a candidate of non-partisan persuasion, so it seemed. It would have been an ideal situation to bring on board an upright independent thinker who would complement the rest and not necessarily fit in with everybody. Already there were several incompetent, and outright charlatans on this campus. It was sad to see the academy being corrupted blatantly, and unchecked.

Valuable colleagues practiced underhandedness and made a mockery of democratic practices in committees. They sprayed a whiff of decaying democracy in America. At a human level, for a faculty member of the opposite view, as I was, there was a general feeling of *schadenfreude* in this group! How far will this trend go, one wondered? Fortunately, I could see the day I would retire. I looked forward to that day when I would have completed three decades of teaching at this institution.

Two of my colleagues, with whom I shared departmental responsibilities were genuinely dear to me. Despite our differences, we respected each other and did not wish any harm to come our way. I had no problem with them just because they were products of archaic training that had presumably deviated from the liberal arts tradition. I believed in the liberal arts tradition where we helped young minds to come up with their own ideas rather than being injected with excitements of impulsive partisan spin. These young students must not get intoxicated with tempting presentations and become a prêt-à-porter audience of cognoscenti. Indoctrinating students is not the same as teaching them to think and develop Socratic methods of articulating counter points. Homer and Shakespeare had much to tell us about how to think and live than Jefferson or Madison! Through new knowledge and discovery, we help young minds to solve problems of society toward what they ought to be, and not what they have been.

Indisputably, I had benefited from working with my colleagues of diverse backgrounds on this campus. I am grateful that at the human level we were polite to each other, at least outside the committees. Having matured and prospered in the changing academe the time was right to make a gradual exit. After completing thirty years of full-time teaching and research at this institution, a well-deserved superannuation would be warranted. Hence, I opted for the Faculty Early Retirement Program (FERP) that enabled me to teach as a part time faculty for five years.

But before we get to that stage, much more was happening in parallel during the latter days of my academic life. It would be disingenuous to the readers if they were to be deprived of the melodrama of intense proportion that can at best be deemed as mentality of a blinkered sibling with her baggage of worms reaped from a dysfunctional home. She was enormously successful in wittingly instilling the social venom that almost annihilated those around her.

VII

So far, the narrative of my time abroad chronicled a pursuit of higher education and the customary activities of the academy. It was, in a nutshell, dedicated to my professional scholarly life, tracking the accomplishments after an eagerly meandering graduate education. There was no indication of a nascent anarchic family life. On that front though, signs were flashing intermittently but curtly after we settled in California. The final drama was played out at our last residence in a resort town that was our fifth home.

It can be called an era of turmoil enacted by rogue relatives. It was supplemented by a substandard midlife crisis. In cultural terms, this era of turbulence eventually led to what is appropriately known as, "dharma of exile." In ancient India, Rama (राम), a legendary king of Ayodhya, was also exiled.

As described in the Bhagavata Purana, Rama was an avatar or incarnation of Vishnu. Most Hindus believed Rama to have really existed just as the historic Jesus of Nazareth and Gautama Buddha. With doubtless historicity, he was a palpable king who ruled from his capital city of Ayodhya in the state of Uttar Pradesh over a large geographical area.

Rama was an extra judicious God incarnate, specifically in Vaishnavism, and in its corresponding scriptures of south and southeast Asia. The details concerning Rama have their genesis in Ramayana, one of the two great epics of India. Born as the eldest son of Queen

Kausalya and King Dasharatha of Ayodhya, Rama was referred to by Hindu scholars as Maryada Purushottama, literally the perfect man. Rama was the husband of Sita. Hindus considered Sita to be an avatar of Lakshmi. Hence, she was the embodiment of perfect womanhood. Together they had endured what a common mortal would go through, with all the life's ups and downs. Particularly, their banishment and separation from loved ones, was so believably normal that it resembled any human being's quandary. It had happened before, it is happening now, and it will likely happen again.

Rama's life was one of flawless observance of prescribed virtues of Hindu dharma. Dutifully, he endured the unforgiving tests of life-threatening exile in the forest. For the sake of his father's honor, Rama abandoned his claim to Kosala's throne to serve an exile of fourteen years in the jungle. His wife Sita and brother Lakshmana, being unable to live without Rama, decided to join him. Hereafter, all three spent the entire fourteen years in exile together.

While living in the forest, Sita was kidnapped by Ravana, the demon king of Lanka—supposedly, today's Shri Lanka. After a long and arduous search for his abducted wife that tested his personal strength and morality, Rama fought a colossal war against Ravana's armies. In a war of powerful magical beings, and greatly destructive weaponry, Rama slayed Ravana and rescued his wife—her honor and soul intact. His nobleness won over Ravana's sinful empire. Having completed his exile, Rama returned home to be crowned King of Ayodhya, his most venerated kingdom. People celebrated that occasion by staging a festival of lights, also known as Diwali. Even today, that signifies the victory of good over evil.

According to this epic divine story, Lord Rama reigned for eleven thousand years and brought an era of perfect happiness, peace, prosperity, and justice known as Rama Rajya. His resolve in searching for his kidnapped wife, Sita, and fighting a terrible war to rescue her was complemented by Sita's absolute devotion to her husband despite enduring Ravana's pressure to capitulate and become his wife. Parallel to Rama and Sita's love for each other, today's warm feelings between husband and wife appears pale and constricted. Sita was totally dedicated and loyal to her husband Rama, irrespective of the pull of clan identity, social coercion, and bullying by family members.

Mortals of today should not be compared to Sita. In fact, today we have fractional lovers; indeed, now we have infidels who can sacrifice their love for each other averted by societal interests, sibling demands, and self-fulfilling prophesy. Many in the modern era, succumb not only by the pull of their family of origin, but accede to their ethnic identity that often proves to be an insurmountable force that necessitates detachment from their marital bonds.

Rama's younger brothers—Lakshmana, Bharata, and Shatrughana—strongly complemented his elder brother's piety, virtue, and strength. All of them belonged to the virtuous class of Maryada Purushottama. They were the avatars of nobility. Rama's goodness and godliness attracted powerful and devoted allies such as Hanuman, the monkey king, and his Vanaras (monkey soldiers) of Kishkindha region. With their alliance, Rama rescued his wife, Sita. The legend of Rama remains a deeply influential and popular folklore in the societies of south and southeast Asia. Rama was revered for his endless kindness, courage, and devotion to religious virtues.

***

Without a doubt, Rama's story has a divine beginning and a moralistic end. King Dasharatha announced to citizens of Ayodhya that he planned to crown Rama, his eldest son, the Yuvaraja. While the news was welcomed by everyone in the kingdom, the mind of one of his queens, Kaikeyi, was poisoned by her wicked maidservant, Manthara. Lacking a Manthara, our life's piety and purity would go untested!

Kaikeyi, Rama's stepmother, and brother Bharata's mother was in the palace rejoicing with the other queens and sharing the happy news of Rama's planned coronation. She loved Rama as her own son; but her mean maid, Manthara, was unhappy. She wanted Bharata to be the king, so she devised a heinous plan to obstruct Rama's coronation.

As soon as the plan was set firmly in her mind, she rushed to Kaikeyi and said, "What a fool you are! The king has always loved you more than the other queens. But the moment Rama is crowned, Kausalya will become all powerful and she will make you, her slave."

Manthara's constant pressure not only poisoned but clouded Kaikeyi's mind and heart. Confused and distraught, Kaikeyi finally asked, "But what can I do to change it?"

Manthara deviously laid out her plan. She had been waiting for Kaikeyi to ask her advice. "Do you not remember that long ago when King Dasharatha, your husband, was gravely wounded on the battlefield while fighting the demons (Asuras), you saved his life by swiftly chauffeuring his chariot to safety? At that time, your husband offered you two boons. You stated that you would ask for those boons some other time."

Kaikeyi readily recalled that. Manthara continued, "Now is the time to demand those boons. Ask Dasharatha for your first boon to make Bharat, your own son, the king of Kosala, and for the second boon to banish Rama to the forest for fourteen years."

Despite being a noble-hearted queen, Kaikeyi was now trapped by Manthara. She agreed to do what her loyal servant specified. Both knew that Dasharatha would never fall back on his words. He would rather perish.

The night before the festivity, King Dasharatha went to Kaikeyi to share his happiness about Rama's impending coronation. But Kaikeyi was missing from her apartment. She was in her anger room, pining. King Dasharatha saw his queen lying on the floor with her breast exposed, hair uncombed, wearing just a skirt, and her ornaments cast away. He gently held Kaikeyi's head on his lap and asked in a caressing voice. "What is wrong my darling?" But Kaikeyi angrily shook herself free and spoke firmly. "You had promised me two boons. Now is the time to grant me those two boons."

Here are my demands, "Let Bharata be crowned as the king, not

Rama. And Rama should be banished from the kingdom for fourteen years."

King Dasharatha could hardly believe what he heard. He was puzzled and shocked. Regaining his poise, he enquired. "What has come over you? What harm has Rama done to you? Please ask for anything else but these."

Kaikeyi stood firm and refused to answer. Dasharatha then fainted and remained on the floor the rest of the night. The next morning, Sumantra, his Chief Overseer, came to inform Dasharatha that all the preparations for the coronation were ready. But his boss was not able to speak to anyone. Instead, Kaikeyi requested Sumantra to call Rama immediately. When Rama arrived, his father was sobbing uncontrollably and could only utter his son's name. "Rama! Rama!"

Rama was alarmed and looked at Kaikeyi with surprise. "Did I do anything wrong, mother? I have never seen my father like this before."

Replied Kaikeyi, "I have something unpleasant to tell you, Rama. Long ago your father had offered me two boons. Now I am claiming those." Then Kaikeyi told Rama about the boons.

"Is that all mother? Please understand that your boons are granted. Let brother Bharata take the throne. I shall start for the forest today." Rama did his pranams (paying respects) to his revered father, Dasharatha, and to his stepmother, Kaikeyi, and then left the room. Dasharatha was hopelessly impaired. Agonizingly, he asked his attendants to help him to Kausalya's apartment where he would now wait for his end.

The news of Rama's exile spread like a fire. Lakshmana was furious with his father's decision. Rama simply snapped, "Is it worthwhile to sacrifice your principle for the sake of this small kingdom?" Tears sprung from Lakshmana's eyes, and he said in a low voice. "If you must go to the forest, take me along with you." Rama agreed. Then Rama talked to his wife Sita and asked her to stay behind and look after his mother, Kausalya.

Sita begged, "Please do not leave me behind. I will die without you. Have pity on me. A wife's place is always next to her husband."

This plea was characteristically Indian, totally unlike a modern woman who would clinch that chance for personal gain and comfort.

At last Rama allowed Sita to accompany him. Urmila, Lakshmana's wife, also wanted to go. But Lakshmana explained to her that the life he plans to lead is for the protection of Rama and Sita. "If you accompany me *Urmila*," Lakshmana pleaded, "I may not be able to fulfill my duties. Please take care of our grieving family members." In the end, Urmila stayed behind on Lakshmana's appeal.

This narrative has a powerful lesson for all of us. Rama realized that a king must neither break a solemn promise at any time, nor a son should disobey his father's wishes. Is it not like marriage vows people take? Rama's wife joined her husband in exile despite his discontent. She considered it her duty to accompany him. She reminded Rama of their marriage vows. Out of love and loyalty for Rama, Sita believed that she must be always at her husband's side. Also, Rama's younger brother, Lakshmana, was determined to join Rama rather than remain in the city.

As they left for exile, the people of Ayodhya were deeply saddened and angered at King Dasharatha and Queen Kaikeyi. Unable to bear the agony of separation from Rama, King Dasharatha who was totally heartbroken collapsed and died the next day.

Rama did not bear any anger towards his stepmother Kaikeyi, believing firmly in the power of destiny. Providence is what controls our life. According to the lessons from our epic Ramayana, this exile presented Rama an opportunity to confront the demon Ravana and his evil empire.

Rama's brother, Bharata, could not believe that his biological mother, Kaikeyi, was the cause of his family's fiasco. She tried to make him understand that she did it all for him. Repulsed, Bharata turned away from her and cried. "Don't you know how much I love Rama? This kingdom is worth nothing without him. I am ashamed to call you, my mother. You are heartless. You killed my father and banished my beloved brother. I will not have anything to do with you as long as I live." Then

Bharata went to be with his stepmother Kausalya. Right then Kaikeyi realized the blunder she had committed.

Kausalya received Bharata with love and affection. She pleaded with him to rise to the occasion. "The kingdom is waiting for you, Bharata. No one will oppose you for occupying the throne. Now that your father is gone, I would also like to go to the forest and live with Rama." Bharata could not contain himself any further. He burst into tears and promised Kausalya to bring Rama back to Ayodhya as quickly as possible. He said he was mortified because his biological mother had coldheartedly brought this calamity. He declared that the throne rightfully belonged to Rama, not to him. After completing the funeral rites for his father, King Dasharatha, Bharata started for Chitrakoot where Rama was staying. Bharata halted his army at a respectful distance and walked alone to meet him. Approaching Rama, Bharata fell at his feet begging forgiveness for all the wrongs done to him.

Embracing his younger brother, Rama inquired about their father. Bharat began to cry and conveyed the sad news. "Our father has left us for heaven," he uttered mournfully. "At the time of his death, he constantly called your name and never recovered from the shock of your departure," he explained. Rama also broke down and tears began to roll down his cheeks. When he recovered, he walked over to the Mandakini River to offer prayers for his departed father. The next day, Bharata asked Rama to return to Ayodhya and rule the kingdom. But Rama firmly replied, "I cannot possibly disobey my father. You rule the kingdom, and I shall carry out my pledge. I will come back home only after fourteen years." Despite the coaxing of royal sage, Vasishtha, and the pleas of his brother, Rama refused to return. Although horrified at the news of his father's death, he was determined to continue his mission.

When Bharata realized Rama's firmness in fulfilling his promises, he begged Rama to give him his sandals. Bharata told his brother that the sandals will represent his rule and the kingdom will be managed in his behalf. Rama graciously agreed. Bharata carried the sandals to Ayodhya with great reverence. After reaching the capital, he placed the sandals on the throne and ruled the kingdom in Rama's name. He himself lived outside the palace in a hut, as Rama did in the forest, counting the days of Rama's return.

After Bharata left, Rama went to visit Sage Agastha, who asked Rama to move to Panchavati, a beautiful place on the bank of the Godavari River. From there on Rama stayed at Panchavati where his brother Lakshmana quickly put up an elegant hut and they all settled down.

***

Between Kaikeyi and her maid Manthara there was a relationship in which the former was controlled and manipulated by her only confidant. Kaikeyi was stricken with a pathological condition which in broader terms refers to the dependency on the needs of, or control of another. Often it involves placing a lower priority on one's own needs, while being excessively preoccupied with the needs of others. This condition can occur in any type of relationship, including family, friendship, clan affiliations, and romance. It may also be characterized by low self-esteem, excessive compliance, and a need to be subservient. A person with this syndrome is not quite sure what she must do in any circumstance, real or imagined. Since it will be what others would have her do, she would not be responsible for the outcome even if it were unpleasant and destructive to her.

Historically, this relationship originated directly out of Alcoholic Anonymous, as part of an emerging realization that the problem was not solely the addict, but also the family and friends that constituted a network. This paradigm was subsequently broadened to cover the way that the affected person was fixated on another person for approval, need, and demand. As such, the concept overlaps with the earlier psychoanalytic concept of the passive dependent persona who attaches herself to a stronger personality type.

Often some people would retain the stricter and narrower dictionary definition of this syndrome, i.e., a person needs to be physically or psychologically addicted, say to a sibling. However, both parties would have to be emotionally dependent on each other.

The dependence of Kaikeyi and Manthara on each other reinforced a mutually harmful behavior pattern; in that, their thoughts and feelings went beyond normal activities of self-sacrifice or caretaking. For example, parenting is a role that requires a certain amount of self-sacrifice by giving a child's needs a higher priority. Although a parent or a caretaker could nevertheless still be mutually needful towards their own children, the caretaking or parental sacrifice at times can reach unhealthy or destructive levels. Generally, a parent who takes care of her own needs, emotional and physical, in a healthy way will be a better caretaker, whereas a chronically needy parent may be less effective or may even be harmful to a child. To put it another way, the needs of an infant or an infantile sibling are necessary but temporary, whereas the needs of the obsessive parents are endless.

People who are mutually dependent on each other often take on the role of a martyr. Not only do they constantly put others' needs before their own, but in doing so forget to take care of themselves or those who are a primary family member, such as a spouse. This creates a sense that they are indispensable and cannot stand the thought of being alone with no one needing them. Pathologically partnered people, such as Queen Kaikeyi and her maid servant, were constantly in search of acceptance. When it comes to arguments, they also tend to set themselves up as a victim; but when they do stand up for themselves, they feel guilty.

This kind of mutually conditional relationship does not refer to all caring behavior or feelings, but only those that are excessive to an unhealthy degree such as changing the course of a family's wherewithal and even survival. Indeed, from the standpoint of attachment theory, becoming needy may be for the compulsively self-reliant a psychological progress. However, depending on a source outside oneself—say, for success, tolerance, reliance—excessive dependence on others may have a phony value.

Let us take this phenomenon one step further: a self-centered person, with her ability to get others to buy into her vision, is a natural base for the co-dependent who has the tendency to put others' need before her own. Codependents, be they a leader and his follower, or two siblings of a flawed family, provide the narcissistic among them with a flattering, unthreatening audience, and a perfect backdrop for further misery. Among the reciprocally locking interactions of the pair, one must look at the way the egotistical one maneuvers an overpowering need to feel important and special. The selfish between the two, amplifies her needs and demands attention from the other. While a co-dependent sister undergoes a sacrificial mode to please her sibling, she does almost no self-caring. She could care less about those who depend on her—say a spouse or a child.

In psychoanalytic terms, the narcissistic who manifests such invincible behavior, and who seems to be especially needy, exerts an opiate in the power equation. They feed and fuel the emotional necessities of the other and benefit through their increased sway. Unresolved patterns of undue dependence or reliance on others can lead to more serious self-defeating behaviors like eating disorder, drug addiction, and craving for intoxicants. Eventually it could lead to a feeling of powerlessness and an acceptance of the inevitably adverse fate.

The consequences of the unseemly dependence that existed between Kaikeyi and her maid, Manthara, were utterly destructive. The grossest outcome was the death of the patriarch King Dasharatha, followed by the exile of the two brothers and the abduction of older brother's wife. The whole family, indeed, the entire kingdom was stressed out. The kingdom was not only destabilized because the people did not know who their king was, but a power vacuum made it potentially susceptible to invasion from the neighboring rival rulers. Eventually, the need to depend on her conniving maid destroyed Kaikeyi herself. Her own son ridiculed and abandoned her for causing such a grievous error of judgment.

***

From here on the author of this pseudo-mythical story which constituted a preface to Dhir Dayal's (Dhir's) narrative shall be conveyed in a third person genre; principally, it was necessitated by his advancing years. Not that he was unable to complete the task, but he wanted to guarantee the story's genuine advancement and its essence via a suitable scribe.

The epic story about Rama's exile enumerated above was composed in response to a prerequisite for Dhir's homework for continuing a short-term counseling. The counselor asked him to compose a metaphor for his feelings of what had transpired in his marital life and how he felt about it and its consequences. The task was to formulate a developing background for the disruption of a seemingly durable marital verve. To cast the historical basis in Dhir's mind was his cultural exposure to an indelible impression that all Indian youth possessed, i.e., a folktale from the epic Ramayana. In his mind the scenario of his impending marital breakup was akin to a "dharma of exile."

All great religions have life's metaphors that are applicable to human lifecycle. The heroic story described above ensues in modern times as well, especially when one marries someone of a different culture, race, and religion. Few people close to Dhir had warned him that after few years the American born and raised woman would want out of her marriage relationship. Lo and behold! It came. It happened. He observed the detachment, the deceit, hidden psychological infidelity, unraveling, and secret conversations with certain church members. Along with that was a devious equivalent to Kaikeyi's maid, a sibling in this case, purportedly prodded by a parent.

Marriage in America appears essentially a license to legally share a living space while having access to each other freely, continuously, and unhesitatingly. Often there is a lot of sharing of values, external and internal. Sometimes it is called love and often we hear people joke about it. Some may call it mutual dependence. When this intimacy becomes a casual affair and a matter of convenience of shared mortgage property, occasional curling in bed, and even sexual intimacy, there is something missing—the original penchants of affinity are diluted, and the bond begins to break. Indeed, then they resort to pragmatic and prosaic tolerance of each other.

The modern-day goals of marriage, security, and comfort are sadly rationed. For many the idea of contented marriage to end is too cozy and tame. New opportunities may arise. People yearn for what should be termed as strenuously exhibitionist happiness or living a secret life of unhappy spouses. Instead of the façade of being simply married they tended to strive to achieve the ingenuous warmth, and waning emotions.

Dhir's broken marriage was several times more sumptuous than other folks' successes. Perhaps that is something we need to admit about failure. It was much more lavish than meager success. Somewhere in their collective unconscious minds they knew that because they had failed to have a genuine relationship more of the same was not normal. Continuous conflict triggered by an officious sibling and resulting disagreements did not seem healthy. Ostensibly, their conscious world saw no utopian healing.

***

In the United States, interracial marriages became legal nationwide on June 12, 1967, after the Supreme Court threw out a Virginia law that sent police into the Loving's bedroom to arrest them just for being who they were—a married Black woman and her White husband. Like Virginia law, one-third of the states went beyond Black and White alliances and prohibited marriages between Whites and Native Americans, Filipinos, Indians, Asians, and in some states all non-Whites. Five years before the widespread prohibition, Dhir and his wife were married in a small town close to President Harry S Truman's home. When the Supreme Court decided the Loving's case in 1967, only three percent of newlyweds in the Unites States were interracial. In 2015, seventeen percent of newlyweds had a spouse of a different race or ethnicity. Today, in this country, one out of ten such married couple is multiracial or multiethnic.

In the initial years, the grandeur of having broken all the usual barriers of race, religion, and culture was a kind of heroism, even if the closeness was neither genuine nor founded on usual sequential events; perhaps, a sense of urgency prevailed to make a go of it. Because their alliance was unconventional and incidental, subtle messages of disapproval were coming from all sides, especially from family members. Some said, "This too shall pass." Others proclaimed that the initial, hyped-up occasional meetings during courtship are not usually carried forward during constantly living together. Most asserted that incompatibility would soon make them go their separate ways. Initially, Dhir did not feel there was any credible reason to sever a novelty in the short run at least. Even if the union did not follow typical norms, it did resemble the predictable ways and means. In one sense, to avoid an abrupt breakdown they initially drifted comfortably along in a dull relationship. But to spend precious years of life in a spurious marriage was neither satisfying nor exciting. Was contentment too ambitious and modest a goal? At the end of the day when we are weary and seek a comfortable bed to recuperate from our exhaustion, is not a warm body next to you recompensing? Is the strength of feeling redeemed in the blaze of a passion worth it, even if it does not end happily?

Despite the prevailing nervous tension, the estranged couple, not knowing how to conduct their daily life, did the usual things that married couples did. They coexisted. Just sleeping together on the same bed can be a temporary break from the doomsday scenario. And talking to each other normally in the company of others was the right thing to do. Even this façade worked for a while. It bought time. But for only so long; in the end the curtain fell, though quietly but decisively!

Close friends who knew about the genesis and the players involved in this drama became alarmed about the frequent visits of his wife's sibling. Perceiving something uncommon about these visits, they asked Dhir about the possible motive of this imposter. His friends suspected that she was up to some sinister plot that possibly might prove to be harmful to him or his unsuspecting family. Hence, they hinted at first and later urged Dhir to stay away when she comes. At a minimum they urged that he should not have meals with them!

VIII

One night in their bedroom, Dhir was awakened by his wife while he was loudly talking in his dream, saying, "No, no, no way." At breakfast, he recalled his dream, in which she was comically comparing the differences in their skin tone—one pinkish gray and the other brown. She exclaimed, "We have nothing in common, do we?"

It was alarmingly dreamlike behavior on the part of this woman. It seemed the idea of race and color, never uttered before, was seething into her mind, no doubt instigated by someone in her circle of contacts—a devil incarnate.

This dream occurred during the early stages of figuring out what the sources of Dhir's marital aberrance were. Certainly, it was a result of confiding in a sibling, who must have insinuated about the different physical appearances of the couple, an observation acquiesced to by the so-called wiser women of the local church. Self-anointed church women are known to pass quick judgment about someone who stays married to a non-Christian. Are such American Christians good role models? Are American women good Christians?

It was known that Dhir's spouse's sister was a racist bigot, based on occasional comments she would make. Their father was often heard uttering the "N-word." So, they had to have learned it from their parents while growing up in the Midwest's hinterland.

From that moment on, the distance between Dhir and his spouse began to get expansive; they went through an all-purpose marriage counseling with a woman pastor. As the counseling progressed, he felt victimized by this counselor, as she seemed biased in favor of his wife's point of view. She suggested that Dhir was the root cause of the conflict. At last, one day, he could not endure her accusations and walked out of her office in total disgust. After that, he knew what the counselor would advise his wife to do.

The following week after her counseling session with Ms. Hoosier, his wife came home and asked Dhir that, for therapy's sake, he rent an apartment temporarily and move out of the house. He did not think of asking, "Why don't you move out?" But then she said she would compensate him for the mortgage payment each month. He fathomed he had suffered enough harassment, hostility, and an implicit threat to his well-being that the move was an easy way to prepare for what might transpire later. Therefore, he consented to the plan of a necessary exile. In the beginning, it seemed easy to live away. He felt good about the idea.

Then a date was set, and they drove to Northridge and told their daughter about their decision to live apart provisionally. What a shock that must have been for a young person. Dhir wondered how his daughter would begin to grasp such a breakup. Would she feel abandoned? How would it feel that her parents were going to live in two different places? How would she cope with her own future? They made sure that, financially, she would be secure. Dhir bought a new car for her transportation. But he saw a psychological change that began to happen in her that manifested as traits of insecurity. His daughter's future began to look gloomy. How would she survive now? Who would take care of her?

When the wife's counselor asked her to tell her husband to move out of their house that he had paid for, his dharma of exile began. As their relationship had been poisoned, his surroundings began to look ugly; psychologically and socially, it felt suffocating. He wanted to make a total break, never to return to this spurious relationship, marred by dishonesty and intervention by a selfish and sinister sister. Immediately in disgust, he rented a comfortable apartment near his campus and moved there.

Imagine that he had to move out of his own home—a home he had designed, had built, and for which he had accepted a thirty-year mortgage. He was told that was a normal practice when American couples become estranged and had to prepare to go their separate ways. To him, that was an alien practice, totally unacceptable in his culture, but it was a fact fully grounded in Western societies. He was here now, not there. Here, most women were empowered in ways that were inconceivable in Asian cultures.

In African tribes, after a husband decides to move out of his house, the woman stays with children and relatives of her choosing. There, too, the husband is cast off. Some men in Africa are delighted to be in that predicament. At first, Dhir was too.

It was remarkable to note that the weekend after he moved out, his wife hosted her sister and her two mischievous sons—known for extracting freebies all the time—for a family get-together, no doubt to celebrate Dhir's departure. At this tragically memorable get-together of the two codependent sisters, reportedly, the younger one suggested to her older sister, "Let us celebrate."

"How do you intend to do that?" asked the older one.

The younger sister replied, "Let's burn your marriage certificate."

"No. Are you crazy? I will need that for the final act."

So, they made a Xerox copy of the certificate and threw it in the fireplace and sang a song: "We shall overcome."

Misunderstanding what was going on, the two insane brothers undertook a contest of pissing in the fireplace and ended up wetting the Turkish carpet nearby. Their mother simply laughed about that whacky scene.

Dhir's daughter arrived home soon after the ceremonial fireworks. Having driven from college, she did not anticipate seeing enthusiasm and glee in her father's absence. She was appalled to see that the occasion was festive. She resented the joyful event the two sisters were reveling in. Sadness overcame her, and a few short hours later, she left her own home in shock, pronouncing to her own mother, "You are not my mother. I am ashamed to call you, my mother. You evicted my father for this—to entertain your sister and nephews! You are heartless. I will not have anything to do with you as long as I live."

The above scenario was a wicked mockery. And who was responsible for this higgledy-piggledy? A sibling. Or was it the head of their family himself? Nevertheless, the timing was right; their daughter was away and attending college in a different town. It was a real comedy in which the loser would be the trapped sister—a sister who had married this man, had a child with him, and slept with him for decades. It was a real mystery as to who was the real cause of this drastic measure. Could it be the fear of sharing the inheritance of the family farm after the death of the old man that was driving this hateful campaign? What was their father's role? He must have known what was going on.

Why allow your daughter to marry someone who will not belong to your circle? Was it a temporary arrangement? Was it to satisfy her unmet carnal desire or to have grandchildren? Men and women have entered matrimonial compacts for at least a millennium, and yet in many cultures, they have not figured out how to care for each other. To have a strong and lasting marriage, a couple must respect their marriage itself as central.

The sanctity of the maternal mindset requires tolerance and a sense of coexistence. Frequently what disrupts it is the couples blaming each other for small and trivial things of daily life. Invariably, women blame men for snoring and commandeering the bedcover. Often the involuntary twitch in a man's knee ends up kicking the woman's hind while they're asleep.

Just because a woman is generally fragile, if not smaller, does not mean she requires less personal space. Men don't realize they cannot shrink themselves; women would not want them to, and their clumsy size and shape are part of men's appeal. Most women seem happy about it. The bigger the better is not to be seen when it comes to negotiating the matter of bed space though.

And for that classic case of sleeping together, before or after their usual routine—forbidden in their case—the spooning was accepted; let the woman initiate. She might say, "Not tonight. Just hold and touch me." There is a chance she might not want to wear a human for a garment.

The act of spooning comes handy in managing the arms and the head. Unless your lady is experiencing hypothermia, she will let your arm rest on her belly. If she pulls your hand from her stomach to her chest, it is because, no matter how much a woman loves being held, she can't be sleeping and sucking in her stomach at the same time. But hey, man, you get to sleep with a hand on her boob, so this is a win for you, especially if the counselor has instructed her not to get too intimate.

In actuality, there may not be such a thing as a committed, balanced, or healthy relationship. Outside forces, old alliances, sibling dysfunctions, and capricious friends have enabled many married women to revile their spouses. Listening to such distractions has contributed to the dissolution of many marriages. It was happening to Dhir's colleagues all the time. As polite listeners, such meek and gullible women must cease to enter romance. It may seem logical to such women that the external guidance is not spurious, self-serving, or injurious. They lack aptitude to distinguish between their own long-term interests and the distractive and destructive self-serving advice of others. How ingenuous can some women be?

Who suffers the most at the end of a chain of events leading to a breakup? Certainly, it does not harm the distracters.

Meddlers have no success with millions of quietly married couples who cannot be targeted. Their attack succeeds with soft marriages— with timid and susceptible people and those who are characterized as bland, loveless, rootless, vulnerable, gullible, and culturally sundry. Strong and self-assured people are aware of these intruders and know how to deal with them.

There definitely was a network of newsmongers and gossip addicts at the university campus where Dhir worked. They shared and selectively gossiped about the marriages, separations, divorces, and even deaths of those who worked there. In Dhir's case, he began to encounter people he had never met or seen before. While walking on campus, especially between classes, he would be greeted. "How are you?" "How are things going?" "Are you OK?" Rarely did he encounter this sort of tuneful "howdy" before.

One morning, a woman stopped him while he was returning to his office from a classroom. She talked as if they had known each other. She said, "I know what you must be going through. You must see a counselor. You need someone who will listen to you. I was talking to your secretary, and I know someone, an excellent counselor, who is very good."

Dhir affirmed, "That sounds like a worthy suggestion."

As he entered his office, the telephone was ringing, and the caller gave him Dr. Frandon's phone number. When contacted, the counselor, who believed in short-term counseling, appeared scholarly, good-natured, and serene. They met once or twice a week. The starting point in counseling was to assess Dhir's state of mind. To that end, the counselor asked him to write an essay, which was portrayed in the previous chapter. That was how the patient felt at the start of his exile, and it set the stage for his counseling. The counselor commended him for his scholarly and anecdotal composition.

During this time, peculiar and uncanny events continued to draw him in. What was bizarre was the visit to his office of an Indian woman claiming to be a fellow professional and looking for a job in his department, of which he was the acting chair. He told her there were no openings, but she did not take no for an answer and came several times just to see him. Each time, she would draw his attention to her breasts. He could tell if she was outside his office and would not respond. At times when she would see him, he would pretend to be on his way to a classroom or a meeting. Later, he deduced who the person might be behind this imposter—his dean, who was a native of New York via Guyana.

Most welcome were the gestures of four and sometimes five of his coed students—single, married, and divorced. On weekends, Dhir would join them on the lawn in front of the library to listen to the spring music ensemble. Some evenings, they would go to his apartment for tea and a meeting in conjunction with the upcoming Model United Nations contest in New York City.

During the Easter break, the day they arrived at the Grand Hyatt in New York City, the students presented him with a lovely teddy bear. These women, no doubt prompted by Dhir's secretary, Ms. Mezzow, were insightful psychologists. They could read his mind to the fraction. Truly, their caring attention brought happiness and restored his confidence in cultured and caring American women.

For an unknown reason, one day, Dhir called his wife to assess her state of mind. She was icy and abruptly informed him that their future relationship did not look promising. That was all he wanted to know. He felt assured that her negative attitude would not stop emerging new friendships and alliances from forming.

On the second day in New York, one of Dhir's students told him about a group of people who had come to see him in the lobby. A middle-aged Indian man, accompanied by his wife and daughter, was waiting for him. He was puzzled, harassed, and annoyed. His students figured out what was happening, and as it was dinnertime, they cleverly escorted Dhir out of the lobby of the Grand Hyatt Hotel.

***

Early in his transfer of residence from his home to an apartment, Dhir received a phone call from a close friend, Bar Barribey, an older gentleman who wanted to come over and see him. He arrived with his wife. They parked their car opposite his unit, and only he went up to the apartment. His wife did not come out of the car for a reason she described later. Dhir must be angry at American women for their misplaced views on relationships. They were taken to an Indian restaurant in town for a long luncheon session, where they explored various subjects.

Barribey was the first person who took Dhir's estranged wife to dinner after he moved out of the house. He wanted to know what had gone wrong. Dhir was not privy to their conversation until now. But

Joanne, Barribey's spouse, told Dhir that his wife's reason for separation was racial, ethnic, and skin color. Joanne told Dhir she scolded this misguided wife, saying, "You are the one who married him! Isn't he the same man?"

Upon hearing that, Dhir was very upset for several days. He knew then that his easy-going attitude toward such a person could never be what it had been before. If racial and ethnic differences, along with his skin color, were the factors that had led to the dissolution of his marriage, how would such a muddied and injudicious woman deal with their adult daughter? He pondered and wondered about the source of her newly acquired mindset. Or had it been there all along because of her upbringing?

In spite of the uneasy estrangement, Dhir and his spouse continued to interact about their daughter's college education, which they financed. Occasionally, they would meet for dinner. It was highly recommended by those who had gone through a similar experience to remain congenial in order to satisfy the psychological needs of their daughter and a peaceful resolution of the future outcome. He remembered going to lunches, sometimes to Southern California beaches, and to Hollywood plays. Once, they went to Hawaii for a week. To him, that was depressing. Clearly, they were disconnected and he did not like all the posturing that it entailed. His wife, for instance, wore her wedding ring on the right finger. Obviously, they were artfully playacting all the time.

Other than the mental marshland described above, life went on as usual, and he continued to be active with his routine. He kept himself quite busy in his academic work, including traveling to conferences. He tried very hard to convince himself that he was happy living by himself in a confined, quiet, and clean apartment. He had not lived like this by himself for twenty-six years. At times, he was lonely and missed his routine at home, even if he and his wife had been estranged, and life had been stressful. Admittedly, he was anxious and very distressed; and on few evenings he could not help but cry out, "Why me? Now what? How am I going to explain this to my mother and brothers, who I defied by marrying a foreign woman?" No doubt he had clashed with them in order to marry this American woman.

Also, it became apparent that, as soon as he would retire, he would leave this alien land for good. It would be a relief to be out of this bad dream and ill-begotten lifestyle.

One day, he received a letter from India informing him that his mom had had a mild heart attack. That added to his already enduring anxieties. His daughter was visiting him in connection with taking possession of her new car, which he had bought for her. While describing to her his mom's heart attack, he began to sob, which shocked her. It also surprised him. He had not meant to display his emotions while she was there.

By the third month of living in an apartment, the fact of his loneliness became known to his estranged wife. She asked if he would like to host her younger nephew, Jeremy, during his summer break for two weeks. Jeremy used the guest room and went everywhere Dhir went, even to his classes—that is, if he was not sleeping and got ready on time. Jeremy's presence was doubly beneficial to him in understanding the dynamics of Andaman Schultz's family. His presence was extremely useful for both of them. Dhir found a younger relative who respected him, and in return, Jeremy obtained a caring uncle. He enjoyed going to weekly concerts in the park and decided to become a music major when he attended a college. His favorite instrument was the piccolo. Family problems were never discussed. Jeremy knew very little about why his uncle was renting an apartment. He was enjoying the geniality around him. Definitely, he was a happy-go-lucky guy.

However, his older brother was different. One time, he told Dhir, "My dad says my mom is the greatest and most notorious controller of human beings that he has ever met or known to have existed."

Jeremy's father and Dhir got to know each other. Once they chatted at a coffee shop and discussed their spouses' upbringing and habits. Jeremy's mother had squandered away a large amount of his savings and kept it a secret. "I am going to divorce her," Jeremy's father told Dhir.

"Clearly, she has been quite destructive for our family." He added, "My wife was never as pathetic as she is now." He kept on referring to her gross appearance, her lack of hygiene, and her misconduct. One wonders why this man would marry her. Surely, he was not as concerned about her grosser aspects of life as with the negative role model she was for his children. He was concerned about the way she had mistreated his children from his first wife, who was deceased. "They are constantly ridiculed and regularly underfed compared to our two boys. My other children stop living as soon as our younger boys show up. She is a savage, despicable devil," he concluded.

One could fully sympathize with the environment the two sisters were raised in. Their predicament had been difficult. Their mother had become terminally ill and unable to take care of herself, much less supervise her two daughters. Then the father became both mother and father. Under that enormous stress, reportedly, he told his daughters that, not only did he not want any trouble from them, but he might also find someone else to take care of them by parceling them out to relatives. Realizing that, they must have been afraid of life as foster children.

Having been unwanted and experiencing a dying mother, the two sisters' discreet anguish must have prompted them to invent survival techniques. They wanted to show their dad that they were exemplary kids so they would be kept at home and not farmed out either to relatives or to an orphanage. Thenceforth, they had to stick together. One of their ingenious tools was to cook up instant excuses for mundane events and bizarre answers to get out of a blamable incident. Also, they could not afford to quarrel with each other.

In a nutshell, the sisters grew up in a very daunting environment that made them lose their childhood; they were forced to grow up fast, have secrets, and not reveal their true feelings. Growing up in this abusive and cast-off mode, the younger daughter ended up selling her soul to the devil and turned into a nasty, conniving monster.

Anyone unknowingly entering this shocking and seemingly ghastly social environment was bound to experience an arduous and demanding life. A marital failure was sure to occur. Having put this puzzle together, it was time for deep rational thinking. Dhir continued to seek exclusive counseling from his therapist, who taught at a local university. They would converse on various cross-cultural topics. It was amazing how a seemingly good-hearted woman, who had openly loved and married a man from a different culture and ethnicity, could be corrupted and tarnished by an evil-minded sibling. Invariably, serious questions arose. "Why would an American girl, born and raised in a deeply racist society in the rural Midwest, marry someone of brown color from a third world country?" Over time, several thoughts surfaced as the counselor went deeper into the matter of poverty, early abuse, the dysfunctional family, lack of appeal, and insecurity, among a host of other topics that were reviewed.

Psychiatrists have proven that some girls feel safer with a stranger than they do with a member of their own race and class because they were mistreated or abused by a relative or close family friend. These women were, no doubt, hurt in the past by one of their own. Indeed, before the marriage Dhir had insisted that he visit the home of his fiancée and meet her parents. Dhir's future wife was totally unwilling to entertain that idea, exclaiming, "There is nothing there!"

Dhir's counselor kept on exploring the family background of his spouse and his family. Repeatedly, he mentioned that people living in a circle of common circumstances have to be in a balanced relationship. He used to share insights popularized by Carl Jung and Alfred Adler.

Carl Jung, a famous psychologist, wrote that one of the most powerful religious symbols was the circle. To him, a circle was one of the great primordial images of humankind, and in considering the symbol of a circle that way, we tend to define ourselves in a group. A circle represents our totality. Everyone within a circle is one unit. If someone is bent on disrupting this circle, it would certainly destroy the mutual relationships of those within this cosmological culture of interrelatedness.

Alfred Adler, another renowned German psychiatrist, stressed the need to understand individuals within their social context. Adlerian experts adopted a radical stance that cuts across the nature-nurture debate. They view the developing individual as he or she creates his or her personality in response to the demands of nature and nurture. Sometimes it is a subjectively created personality that is unique. An average person is able to create his or her own self-development and its social meaning. Adler identified it as a phenomenon of social worth. The well-being of humanity is expressed in terms of belonging, feeling right, and making a positive impact in the universal mindfulness.

Adler was a pioneer in the area of holistic theory of personality, psychotherapy, and psychopathology. He underscored that people will be more productive when they are encouraged to cultivate feelings of adequacy, respect, fulfillment, and hope. Expressions that bring out positive influences encourage our feelings of fulfillment and hope. Adler held strongly that a misbehaving child is a rejected child and that children's behavior patterns improve most significantly when they are supplied with feelings of acceptance and admiration. When parents ridicule their children, they are crafting them into damaged goods. Also, inferiority and inadequacy can be a result of birth order, especially if the youngster was bombarded with derision at an early age. The Adlerian therapist who was helping Dhir paid special attention to emerging belief systems and the behavior patterns that develop all through childhood. Indeed, a child's role should be examined, he asserted, as a member of a circle. Is a child integrated in the family circle?

In Sanskrit, the word for circle is mandala. A mandala is symbolically designed so it has the meaning of an extraterrestrial order. While composing mandalas or a system of relationships, ancient Hindus tried to coordinate their personal circle with the universal circle. There is a deity in the center, serving as the source of power, the supplier of illumination. The peripheral images would include their noble ancestors' manifestations, along with other deities' radiance. Malicious energies with demonic goals will always try to enter this circle and be a source of destruction for this unit. So, the goal should be to detect and undercut that negative force. In acute cases, those energies ought to be emasculated for the sake of others' survival. That was the intention of Dhir's counselor in rescuing him from an impending harm that might occur.

Overall, the Adlerian approach to psychotherapy clarifies that all life confronts potential obstructions, and therefore, attaining good life overcomes those obstructions. Around the center, good and bad forces may float. But when everyone in a circle is properly connected, it is a tranquil circle that not only keeps each person peaceful but also keeps the bad forces in check. But Dhir's circle, because of the evil interference, was in turmoil.

In actuality, while building a relationship through marriage, we are forming a mandala. We are portraying a circle and then imagining different impulses and value systems that become universally acceptable wisdom in our life. Then we strengthen our circle and try to find the true center that all can relate to. Making a mandala or a circle requires discipline. It necessitates pulling all those scattered aspects of our life together. Finding a center and ordering ourselves to it should be our goal. That way, we can strive to harmonize our inner circle with the outer circle and attain peace and stability.

Invariably, cross-cultural unions, burdened with identities of race and ethnicity and educational and economic disparities do create negative energies. Because they dispel common interests and lack similar social terrain, a disruption in relationship is sure to occur. All of these can be traced to the variabilities in the participants' socialization. However, an alert and caring circle of relatives could avert any inappropriate inequity.

Because of the polluted circle caused by the phobic meddling of a sibling, the effect of this marital estrangement was impacting their own daughter. For years, Dhir was plagued consciously that his cherished offspring was unjustly blamed by her own mother for incidents she was not responsible for, like broken cups and dirt and debris. This used to happen when her mother's sister would bring her overindulged "boys." The sister wanted a lot of money spent on these boys because they were deemed superior to girls in their misogynistic extended family. In reality, there was no basis to their claim that boys were superior in their clan.

They were ordinary fellows. In fact, girls did much better, though mental illness was not uncommon. Of three men in their father's family, only he completed a high school education and was gainfully employed as a farmer. His other two brothers stayed home and never had their own families. In other words, they never grew up and remained freeloaders. Hence, it was a myth that, in their family, boys were superior to girls.

A very peculiar thing about Dhir's spouse was that, though she was a nurse, a health-care giver, she hesitated to take her own sick child to a doctor. One evening after Dhir had returned from work, his daughter, who was just five years old, came to him staggering and mumbled, "Daddy, I am sick!"

That broke his heart. Immediately, he called his physician at his home at sunset and asked his advice. The doctor told him to take the child to the hospital emergency department. "And tell them you are new in town and need a doctor to see your daughter."

A doctor on duty admitted this sick child and promptly put her in an oxygen tent. She was suffering from pneumonia. This incident captured the extent of the dysfunctionality of this mother's family. Coming from such a home environment and having endured the absence of a protective mother, how would she, as a mother, cope with her own child and with life?

Ostensibly, these sisters came from a home with no female role model. In the absence of a caring mother, who would be the daughter's role model? Growing up normally was not guaranteed for her. She grew up in a virtually broken and damaged home. One always hates the term "broken home." It sounds so negative, so dented. How can one not revile the term when it lives up to its name? No doubt, Dhir was more concerned about his daughter than he was about himself. After moving into an apartment, he felt that not only had his family life been smashed, but also something inside of him had been wrecked. Days later, he understood a great deal about insecurity and pain, not that it had been absent when his spouse was developing estrangement and creating a space for herself.

Living alone in the apartment, he was at peace most of the time. Some days, he missed his home and thought it was an unjust maneuvering. His moving out was the result of an unfair American custom, and yet it was a great relief from the constant tension and the irritation of his sister-in-law's continuous visits. Now there was no weekly invasion by her and her two spoiled brats, who fought each other all the time. For that reason alone, it had been hard for him to concentrate on preparing his lectures for the following week. Now, in his apartment, there was peace and tranquility. Here, he could serenely make plans for a book without the impish boys running up and down the stairs. At home, he did not get any support for his work. His was not a nine-to-five job. As a scholar and a professor, he deserved a quiet home environment. His sister-in-law's recurrent visits were not just an imposition but also a burden in an already wrecked home—a wreckage of which she was the main architect. Could they have avoided the source of a horrific strain short of breaking their home environment? Not when the sisters were in a codependent relationship.

Unlike his spouse, Dhir was closely and intensely linked to his parents and brothers, along with significant relatives in his circle of well-wishers in India. He had a very strong support system and could not underestimate the impact of parental separation and resulting specific problems that would plague his adult daughter. He ascertained that parental estrangement contributed to problems with children's self-concept, self-confidence, self-worth, and ability to have successful relationships.

The new behavioral sciences have brought us a great deal of literature about the problems of broken homes. Young people invariably carry into adulthood the template of the relationship they observed between their parents. It can become a framework for their new families. The absence of a good image would negatively influence his daughter's search for love, intimacy, and normal commitments. Anxiety led many young adults into making bad choices in relationships, resorting to hasty options without ensuring their long-term interest and security.

One noted scholar followed a group of children from the affluent Marin County, north of San Francisco, whose parents were divorced.

She continued to interview her subjects long into their adulthood. Her findings were astonishing. The researcher unexpectedly found that children were plagued by their parents' divorce many years after it took place, even as adults with families of their own.

To Dhir, that finding was bewildering because the common belief of the last few decades had been that, while divorce may have a negative effect on young children, when these children became adults, the past adverse effects would likely dissipate. New studies revealed this was not the case. One scholar found that children of divorced parents struggled on a long-term basis. Many of their issues centered on their inability to develop healthy relationships. Most of the subjects were consciously aware of the negative effects of their parents' estrangement, with or without a divorce. But with many concerned offspring, the changes are often innate, leaving them upset and puzzled as to why they responded to certain situations in unhealthy ways—such as getting married at the first chance to an incompatible partner.

This evidence had an extraordinary meaning for Dhir, and he wanted to make a decision that would not necessarily result in his own personal happiness. Learning about numerous case studies triggered many haunting dreams for him. Often, he would shiver to realize that lecherous stepfathers could become involved in children's life and injure them irreparably. Even knowingly, the mothers would keep quiet because they valued their new marriage more than their own children. Did it validate what divorce supporters were saying—that kids were hearty and could do just fine after their parents' divorce? No. They could not. Even though these wounded souls might survive their parents' disintegration, there would not be a moment—a birthday, a Thanksgiving Dinner or a Christmas—that they would not wish their parents could have made it work. The hollowness of having a fractured family would haunt Dhir's daughter too. Oh, she looked resilient and effectual as of now. But there was no doubt in his mind that her life would be so much better if her parents had given her the legacy of a healthy and intact family life.

Dhir's skilled therapist, along with his well-wishers, especially the older couple mentioned earlier, gave him a clear and practical alternative to his dilemma. Bar Barribey, with whom he was in fellowship at the local Methodist Church, told him that, afterward, he was bound to meet someone about whom he would not know as much—certainly, not where she had been! That was a thoroughly incisive food for thought. A similar way of thinking was offered by a religious man, also in the circle of his friends. He was a beguiling, wise man who was not only from Dhir's cultural milieu but who also understood the possible antidote for this couple's dilemma.

The occasional aggravation he suffered from was not about to vanish because his mind was preoccupied with senseless interfering. Often, thoughts of resentment were finding a fertile ground in his psyche. Lord Buddha, and surely Christ too, taught that "holding on to anger is like grasping a hot coal with the intent of throwing it at someone else; you are [as no doubt Dhir was] the one getting burned." Therefore, his close friend, Dr. Reverend Mike Samarini, helped him release his anger through a ritual. Dhir was asked to write his grievances on chits of paper and throw them mindfully in a fire pot at the altar of his Episcopal Church in that college town.

These two guardian angels, Mr. Barribey and the reverend, agreed that the church therapist who counseled him and his wife in the early stages may have caused the physical separation as a crude and unnecessary tool to mend the ailing relationship. Dhir's own counselor exclaimed precisely the same contention in much more scholarly terms; he diagnosed the source of ailment correctly. Everyone agreed that the goal should not have been to blame, or shame estranged couples. When the incorrectly tutored woman counselor began to point her finger at the man as if he was the primary cause of the estrangement, he had every right to walk out of her office. When a counselor becomes partial and prejudicial, he or she becomes redundant to the ailing couple. Yet the wife was induced to continue her appointments with the pastor without the husband. She remained under the unsavory counselor's charge for quite some time.

Genuine marriage counselors should spend their energy encouraging couples to learn the skills they needed to stay married for a lifetime. For untrained therapists who have their own baggage of misplaced identities, such as their own parents' breakup, the job of counseling others can be an unethically complicated task. It can, no doubt, be an unprofessional errand surreptitiously instigating a biased agenda. This untrained pastor-therapist was prejudiced against men because her father had abandoned her at an early age.

Just around that time Dhir's sister-in-law called in a jovial tone one evening at his apartment, informing him that her sister was seriously thinking of divorce and that he should be warned. It was shocking to hear this news, though her motives were questionable. She was divorced from her husband and no doubt wanted her sister to join the ranks. She was being an evil woman! Her speech carried in it a chilled, whiny tone and the robotic numbness of a mind without feelings of regrets. She thought of herself, her advantages, and her interests only. Mindlessly, she pursued her plots to gain an advantage over her sister's vulnerabilities.

At that moment, Dhir was resigned to his destiny. Whatever happened would be appropriately dealt with. When it happened, he would deal with it because we are not alone in our efforts to support or dissolve marriages.

His wife continued her counseling, and what direction it was headed—toward a total breakup as the sister hoped or a reconciliation for her own security or something else—was not known. Dhir was surprised when, three months after their separation, his estranged wife began to leave messages on his phone as "Mrs. D." Once, she asked if Dhir would accompany her to a niece's wedding in Arizona.

At the wedding of her cousin, all her close relatives must have seen the telltale signs of trouble, especially because the wife wore her wedding ring on her right-hand finger. That was a giveaway. Also, they were still not supposed to get intimate as commanded by her counselor. Dhir kept on hoping someone would ask, "Why are you wearing your wedding ring on the wrong finger?" But no one said anything. Were they not the meddling kind? Maybe they were confused.

On a drive through the countryside in Arizona one afternoon, the wife shared the bad news about her job being terminated. Not only did Dhir listen to her sympathetically, but he could also sense that a major change in her attitude was in the making. It would be interesting to see what her next move would be. Perhaps she would bring up the topic of her not being able to pay the mortgage.

Thereafter, the wife began to spend a lot of time in his apartment rather than at home. One time, she stayed for five days. Not having located her sister at home, the officious sibling must have panicked and tracked her down at Dhir's apartment. She called him and asked, "Do you know where *she* is?"

Dhir chuckled and sardonically uttered, "Yes. She has been here for five days."

The caller blew her fuse, and one could hear how loudly she was shouting at her sister on the phone, "What are you doing there? No, No. You should not be there. Go home!"

Dhir was amused listening to her furiously scolding her sister for being with her separated husband.

Although most of the time she was guarded, she was not this time. Things were not going her way. Two days later, she must have had a second thought and angrily called Dhir one evening, enquiring, "How often does my sister come there?"

Dhir was annoyed and replied, "That's none of your business."

After a pause, she screamed in a harsh tone, "I wish you would vanish—be dead!" She hung up before Dhir could say anything.

It was wise that he did not call her back and yell at her. Given the nature of codependency between the sisters, it would have further complicated the matter. So, he discussed that obnoxious phone call with his counselor.

The therapist was alarmed hearing that, and he made his client fully understand the intensity of the problem. Although he listened calmly and intently, he became very pensive and slow in verbalizing his thoughts. Dhir's interaction with his counselor, Dr. Frandon, was extremely Socratic and educational. He was a teacher as well as a healer. He revealed the pros and cons of the predicament Dhir was in at that stage of his life and his professional career. Dr. Frandon began to cautiously prepare his client for the ultimate dissolution of this marriage. He was a very thoroughly practical yet cerebral counselor who got to know all components of this loop—the client, his spouse, the sister-in-law, and his daughter.

At this stage of his client's life, based on prevailing feelings about his job, a precious daughter, and his hope for normalcy, the counselor also wished that a congenial approach toward life be pursued, if possible, provided his spouse was also moving in that direction. All of this was left for deep meditation, resulting in maintaining a genial fabric of married life.

His suggestion was to have a meeting of the two counselors and their clients. To that end, Dr. Frandon tried calling Ms. Hoosier, the other counselor, for at least a month. He continuously tried to contact her but to no avail. The latter did not return his phone calls. Finally, one evening, per chance, Dr. Frandon called Ms. Hoosier at 11:00 p.m., and the latter answered.

At last, a meeting of the two counselors and their clients was arranged. At the meeting, the estranged wife declared, "I have resolved all the issues with [my husband] except that he does not like my sister."

Was this crucial matter about the third person not known to her own counselor?

Dr. Frandon's reaction was, "What does the sister have to do with this marriage?"

Ms. Hoosier replied that her client had a codependency problem. For Frandon, life had certain core priorities, he emphasized. For a marriage to stay healthy and succeed, the couple must put their own family's interest first. He had coached his client to make and adhere to a list of priorities—family, work, relatives.

After that joint meeting when Dr. Frandon saw his client the following week, he warned him and cautioned him about getting back in this marriage at this time. He wanted to meet his estranged wife to explore few issues. At the same time, he reiterated to his client that it was important not to make a hasty decision. In this case, he advised his client that, potentially, there was a probable danger of physical harm to him, even death. If the imposter felt betrayed, she might become desperate. Two weeks later, after meeting his spouse, he discussed the alternatives and indicated to Dhir that, for now, the coast may be clear to make plans cautiously, provided certain conditions were met.

He emphasized the prerequisite—in other words, it was absolutely essential for Dhir to arrange a meeting with his wife's sister and make it abundantly clear to her that there should be no interference by her in her sister's marriage. This meeting did take place one-on-one. At the moment, it appeared that she understood his demands. But she had her own cryptic agenda.

***

Exactly six months to the day of leaving, Dhir moved back to his residence. He still remembers the expression on his spouse's face that evening when she arrived home after work. Dhir was unable to forget that blank and awkward expression on her face when she saw him greet her from the porch. Earlier that day, Dhir had taken the delivery of a brand-new bed. Everything had to be new in his mind. They must start afresh.

With that beginning, would they succeed in putting all that had transpired in the past and move on to a new chapter? It seemed extremely difficult because they had different counselors and had been taught different skills. As mentioned before, Dr. Frandon helped his client make a list of priorities; family was on top. He placed that list on the refrigerator, though it disappeared when his wife's sister was scheduled to visit. From there on, she began to visit every other week. Her meddling did not stop. Actually, its frequency increased. The newly reconciled couple had a very rocky time in the early months after they got back together.

Dhir wished neither to go over the sources of postseparation estrangement nor to endure the repeat of discord this meddler had caused in this relationship. There was something quite mysterious happening uncontrollably. To this day, Dhir does not fully understand the minutiae of his spouse's early developmental years; he could only make an educated guess based on their family dynamics and the facade created around the probable prompter responsible for all these happenings. The person behind the two puppets who were engaged in an elusive drama remained a mystery.

After a few weeks, when the meddling did not stop, Dhir became alarmed that things had really not changed. They had the potential to get worse. He realized the sister was up to something ominous when her visits became more frequent. Decidedly, she was the most shadowy person one could meet—a cold, scheming, selfish witch! All that mattered was her interest, her advantage, her everything. Dhir's wife was her responsibility, and she wanted to know everything she did. Why? Such a person could not possibly have scruples. It began to appear that her motives were to have total control of her sister's belongings. She was, no doubt, planning to execute a sinister plot. As a precaution, Dhir would either skip the meal or eat after everyone else had.

Dhir's daughter once asked what her daddy thought of coming back home after a six-month hiatus. His answer was, "I am not sure because things seem to be getting worse than they were before in a different way."

The meddler's ex-husband had told Dhir once, "My wife is an obsessive controller, and I don't wish to deal with her. As huge as her body parts are, her greed is even huger. She is a selfish jerk."

That was a statement Dhir agreed with; she was planning for her sister to name her as the sole inheritor of their California property. She always referred to their California home as "her sister's home." Her primary goal was to eliminate all hurdles in her way, and she was certainly looking for a chance to accomplish that.

***

In the meantime, something far-reaching was to happen that would change the purported scenario. An unexpected misfortune fell upon them that would change the predicted outcome. Their father died. With that death, when his property had to be divided up, noticeably all hell broke loose. The sisters were supposed to divide up the property equally, as per their father's wishes. Indeed, their father asked them repeatedly if he should do that while he was still alive. But the younger sister assured him, "Daddy, we will do it ourselves."

Surely, she had something else in mind. Obviously, her plan was to secure for herself as much as she could. First, the day after his death she commandeered her father's bank account. Then she moved into his farmhouse and did not want anybody around. She wanted it all; at least, she would decide who got what. She wanted the house because, as a divorcee, she did not have one of her own. Ostensibly, these sisters had had a seriously flawed upbringing. Dhir began to sympathize with both! The least he could do was to have pity on them.

The day before their father's funeral, Dhir saw how the evil sister not only seized the farmhouse but also became the controller of everything in sight. Dhir remembered the strangeness of the evening he arrived at his father-in-law's home for the funeral, scheduled for the following day. He saw his sister-in-law having a fit, erratically shouting about all sorts of things. She made sure everyone knew she was now in charge of everything. Loudly she declared, "I don't want to see any man around here."

Of course, Dhir and his wife were invited to sleep at the home of the woman who had taken care of his father-in-law. Everyone kept mum in response to the outrageous behavior of the younger sister because no one wanted to make matters worse at the time of this deific funeral.

Subsequently, it became obvious that, as the relationship between the two sisters deteriorated after the death of their father over the division of his property, at least Dhir was not on his sister-in law's radar anymore. Now she had much more to do to undo her sister's integrity and get an upper hand when it came to what had belonged to her father. Apparently, she took advantage of their father's unspecified general will.

What she was waiting for fell into her lap; she took over not only her father's home and his bank account but also his farm. From there on, the division of their father's property between the two sisters was not an easy undertaking. In a dramatic posture, the younger sister began to terrorize everyone around her, especially her older son. She kicked out his wife because she was Jewish. It was alarming to people around this family that, indeed, this woman had gone mad. But she was just playing an effective role in her well-scripted opera.

Dhir kept on reminding his wife that she had a daughter of her own, and she should not make any compromises with this self-centered person. Gradually, his wife saw the deception and wizened up. But it was a bit too late; the damage was already done. Dhir's spouse cleared barely one-fourth, far less than her share, of her father's assets, totaling more than a hundred acres of prime farmland with a house, a steel storage yard, and two barns. Also, the farm had twenty-two acres of hardwood trees—poplar, walnut, sycamore, oak, aspen, birch, maple, and hickory. The sale of these alone would have fetched no less than $150,000.

In the end, rather than the entire property being divided between the two sisters as their father purportedly wished, it was apportioned into four. This rogue sister parceled out 25 percent each to her two sons. The remaining 50 percent was what the two sisters had available for themselves. The older son, allegedly, used his share of the funds to pay off a huge credit card debt, put the remainder in a savings account, and joined the army. The younger son used his share judiciously; he utilized it to start a trucking business in Texas. So, who took in excess of three-fourths of the proceeds from the sale of a fully endowed farm? The rogue sister did. She was blinded by her greed, to the extent that her own caring sister and her niece did not matter. It was a most notable betrayal of trust in a so-called upright Midwestern rural family.

Clearly, the older sister was swindled by her own deviously precious sibling. This would not have happened if their father had insisted on dividing his property evenly while he was still alive. But his younger daughter, taking advantage of the naivete of her sister, insisted that was not necessary. All self-centered people are denuded of the capacity to think of the consequences of their actions. In fact, women in general are the worst enemy of other women; principally, it is more so when sibling rivalry is rooted in their psyche.

This tacky and selfish sister of Dhir's wife turned out to be his liberator by happenstance. It was she who, by her unabashed treachery, opened Dhir's wife's eyes and made her grasp her gullibility. She came to her senses. She felt hoodwinked. Her low-grade sister was certainly an antihero; a bitch-witch though she was, she knew how to be a loving sister until it was time for the "getting" game. To dwell on this creature is of no benefit; it is better to acknowledge what we can learn from a malicious person and move on.

Under normal circumstances, we do not realize that evildoers can work a lot of good in this fucked-up society. In this case, the sad fact was that the sisters' old man not only could have perceived of the crumbling of his family but probably also knew the source of that spectacle. Even then, he did not reprimand his unruly daughter. Perhaps this revealed the root of the dysfunction this family was tormented by. There was secrecy, hatred, and prejudice. One is not born with these pathologies. So, if people can instill evil ideas in others, those ideas can also be defused. But people in the midst of chaos are unable to acquire prudence and see the evil it unleashes on their own loved ones—the most victimized, as well as the culprit.

Causes and effects of marital injury, in this case, were self-inflicted. One cannot argue whether these ill effects could have been avoided. Deliberating upon this now seems academic only. Learning about what could have been done to build a strong marriage now makes better sense. Dhir simply wanted to remember the obvious—divorce hurts children. As a result, authentic parents should do everything possible, he believed, to heal their marriage.

Notable researchers have explained that even bad marriages become functional over time if the relationship was founded on mutual grounds and not on a fixed goal. Then the marriage is a genuine liaison between just the two. And the experts have argued that married people who have children are happier, healthier, and better off financially in the long run. Social scientists have concluded that a bad marriage is not a fixed fact. They have defined a bad marriage not as those containing abuse and violence but, rather, as those that have ordinary afflictions— sibling meddling, friction over differences in value systems, certain peculiar goals, or the partners' upbringing. Some people are inherently malevolent.

Experts have also argued that, if normal marriages did not end in divorce, they actually improved over time. Just as good marriages go bad, bad marriages can become well, provided both parties make a sincere effort. Sometimes even the motive for survival can do the trick. That is just what Dhir and his spouse did. However, the troublemaker, the meddling sibling in this case, got all she wanted in the form of a greater share of inherited property and went recluse.

All married couples can benefit from learning how to communicate effectively, trust each other, resolve conflicts, and remove meddlers at the outset by building intimacy. Also, the purpose of constructive counseling should be to show every couple how to go about creating trust and affection. The key word is *priority* because a man and his wife come first.

Contrary to what many people believe, even volatile couples can learn to have healthy relationships if they truthfully learn the skills to communicate. Marriage is hard work; it is not a transaction, pure and simple, and all couples can benefit from learning how to do this hard work if they honestly face the alternatives. All this depends on their initial purpose for entering into this institution.

These codependent, miserable sisters were not only raised in a dysfunctional family, but they were also prone to putting the interests of their family of origin ahead of their marriage. This was the conclusion Dhir's counselor expected him to understand and then proceed with his final decision.

An interracial espousing that does not have a problem on either side is atypical. If it's out there, it is someone else's problem. But if your own daughter is in it by marrying a foreign student, then you have to confront your own internal demons. Sooner than later, your own prejudices and aversions will be discovered. It is really hard for some people to accept, on a long-term basis, a spouse from a different race or ethnicity. It was one of the unseen factors behind the drama that was being played out. If not, why did their father not stop this chicanery? What was he afraid of? Was he troubled by his own bigotry? Or was he fearful of being accused of something surfacing from his daughters' childhood that he could not stomach? Who knows? And no one should care!

No doubt, it has been a life's lesson well learned on how we perceive and avoid being affected by the systemic, irrational behavior of those close to us and how our lives are continuously reshaped by past events. In a family network, what some call a "circle," if someone is pathologically destructive of others and causes serious and enduring harm to anyone, every person suffers the consequences of that improbable transgression!

Sadly, we do not take care of our mentally ill. Chronically challenged mental health patients are at the mercy of their parents, schools, churches, and officials who shirk from making the right public policies. When public institutions close all the mental health facilities, putting thousands of mental health patients out on the street, the new patients have nowhere to go for help. So, they fall back on their families and wreak havoc in their circles. On a daily basis, mental illness causes insurmountable social and psychological wounds. If family members who are aware of a disturbed person among them choose to keep quiet, the whole entity suffers and eventually breaks down.

For the newly resurrected couple, the clearest remedy was to sever the relationship completely and sharply with the injudicious person who had been a source of distress, heartache, and extra expense. In this case, the offender herself became a recluse and protective of her loot. That turned out to be the only way to uphold sanity and slowly begin to cauterize the deep wound.

So, at last, the time arrived when Dhir and his wife could build and re-create an environment of congeniality and aim for concord. Dhir's counselor was able to convince him that sometimes it takes a heroic effort to create a functioning family. Indeed, there was just one living being who was of utmost importance to them. Therefore, the best way to be a great father to his daughter was to figure out how to love her mother genially. Hence, it was his earnest desire to reengage and bring normalcy into his life for the benefit of those who mattered.

IX

When Dhir started his career in the late 1960s, it was a critical epoch for America, exemplified primarily by race riots and extremist student activities on college campuses. Even the 1970s were largely unsettling due to the deteriorating quality of life, predominantly triggered by air pollution in all of Southern California, where it was reaching perilous levels. Many gainfully employed professionals were moving toward the mountains to escape harmful air pollution. Some faculty had already moved to a small ski resort at eight thousand feet that was about a half hour drive from the campus. Dhir, too, followed that path and bought a piece of land there and had a split-level, three-bedroom home built while still living near his workplace. Things were not typical. Rapid changes were taking place worldwide.

In 1973, the oil-rich Arab countries organized a cartel called OPEC (Organization of Petroleum Exporting Countries) that rapidly increased the price per barrel of crude oil. Immediately, gasoline prices shot up to seventy-five cents a gallon instead of nineteen or twenty cents. Many professors, who had already moved to higher grounds and were commuting twenty-six miles to campus, could not imagine the future of gasoline prices. Millions of Southern Californians, who also drove long distances to work, saw a doomsday ahead.

Dhir's newly built house in the mountain was close to his daughter's school. After several months, the family felt uneasy living in this small house and did not like the crowding in a congested part of town and right across from a contractor's yard. He used to look up on the other side of town, the sunny side. Hence, he bought a lot there. Two years later, in 1976, the old house was put on sale, and they lived in a rental cabin for a year until their new home in the secluded part of town was ready to be occupied. It had spacious rooms appropriately situated, with a panoramic view of the village below. Upstairs had the living room, their daughter's suite, and the kitchen. This new home became their permanent abode, where they lived for close to three decades, the longest they had lived anywhere.

Living at a ski resort, where the population was slightly over a thousand in 1974 (lately more than ten thousand), they had snow during the winter months (November to March), and the temperatures were ten to fifteen degrees cooler than in the valley below. Although the air was thinner at such an elevation, the fresh air and the blue sky were definitely a boon. But there was a price to pay; essentially, everywhere one had to go was at least a thirty-mile drive.

Friends and associates were very valuable to them. They cherished their friends and confidantes, especially if they happened to be from India. By and large, one could rely on them. When they settled in their new home, they were contacted by an Indian couple, Seeta and Kenny Kishore. Later, while attending an Indian social event at a nearby university campus, they met Aloka Punitam and others. Aloka went to India to get married and brought his new bride, Neelum. Now there were six of them in a close network for social gatherings. Later, Dhir came across Pochy Meherwala from Mumbai, who was enrolled on campus. He was very well appreciated because he helped them move whenever they changed residences. In fact, he and his friends rented a home in the same town. A few times when Dhir was passing through Mumbai, he stayed at the home where his mother and a brother lived. In turn, Pochy's mother visited them a few times.

A notable trip to India took place in connection with the reelection of Indira Gandhi as the new prime minister of India. Earlier in 1975, she had declared a state of emergency for a period of twenty-one months, which was approved by the president of India and ratified by the cabinet and the parliament. It was one of the most controversial periods of independent India's history. Under Article 352 of the Constitution, it was to curb the prevailing internal disturbance. For much of the emergency rule, most of Indira Gandhi's political opponents were imprisoned, and the press was censored. Human rights violations, such as forced sterilization, were carried out by one of the prime minister's sons.

Political opponents challenged the emergency rule. Allahabad High Court found Indira Gandhi guilty, declared her election null and void, and removed her from her seat in the Lok Sabha (House of the People). Indira Gandhi challenged the Allahabad High Court decision. But a higher court upheld the earlier ruling and ordered all privileges she received as a member of parliament to be discontinued. She was also barred from voting. Following that, general elections were held in 1977 to elect the members of the Sixth Lok Sabha, and curiously, the elections were held while the emergency was still in force. The election results were announced before the emergency rule expired.

The outcome was a heavy defeat for the Indian National Congress (INC) and Prime Minister Indira Gandhi. The call for revoking the emergency and restoration of democracy was considered to be the major reason for the sweeping victory for the new leaders. They reactivated the multiparty front, which campaigned as the Janata Party and pushed anti-emergency sentiment to secure a clear majority in the Lok Sabha. Janata Alliance leader Morarji Desai, at age eighty-one, was sworn in as the fourth prime minister of India in March 1977.

Desai's government, from its inception, became notorious for its schism and ferocious internal competition. True to its promise, the Janata government restored freedom and democracy, but its inability to produce sound reforms or even alleviate poverty left people disappointed. Before a no-confidence motion was about to be introduced in parliament, Desai resigned. His government was replaced by a coalition led by Chaudhury Charan Singh, but he too failed to mobilize the coalition. His age and ineptitude were used against him, and his aimless attempts to govern

India failed. New elections were announced, and another opportunity arose for the old power brokers to field their candidate. Indira Gandhi made a run for it.

Gandhi renamed her party Congress I (I for Indira). She vigorously campaigned on the slogan, "Elect a Government That Works"! She regained a majority in the parliament. People were stunned by her energy and her reach to every constituency in India. Also, she extended her influence abroad to the Indian diaspora, who believed in her for fighting for India's reincarnated agenda of national development, eliminating poverty, and restoring decorum.

One of her incoming colleagues, Mrs. N. Malhotra, who was elected as a member of parliament, traveled to the United States and Canada, and contacted key diaspora community leaders who had supported Indira Gandhi's vigorous campaign efforts. She met Dhir in Los Angeles, where he was a newly elected chapter president of the Association of Indians in America. At a dinner meeting in Hollywood attended by about twenty-five local professional and business community members of Indian diaspora, she thanked them for their vigorous backing, praise, and support for Mrs. Gandhi. She remarked that, having been given a chance, the opposition leaders could have produced the needed goals for India. But they failed. Now was the time for us to go back to where we had started from, with a recharged, progressive leader, and make a difference.

Within weeks of Mrs. Malhotra's return to New Delhi, Prime Minister Indira Gandhi's office sent a directive to the San Francisco consulate to invite Dhir and his close friends to meet her in the prime minister's office on a certain date at ten in the morning to discuss their agenda.

With three other members of Dhir's delegation from California, a meeting was held with the prime minister in her office; the meeting lasted about an hour. It seemed important for members of the diaspora to see their motherland not only prosper but also have a good image abroad. Mostly, they focused their questions on India's future goals.

Because the Western press was writing about India's bent toward

Russia, Dhir asked the newly elected leader a question about whether it was a good idea for India to take the side of the Soviet Union. To this the prime minister looked right at him and said, "Professor, we are not pro-USSR or pro-USA. We prefer to be pro-India."

Those gathered were stunned by such a definite and prompt reply. India was certainly in good hands with a leader like Gandhi.

***

Outside of his profession, the circle of Dhir's rapport was widening. Early in the 1980s, he was fortunate to meet and have lunch with a well-known philosopher and teacher, Mr. J. Krishnamurti (JK), during his annual visit to his residence near Santa Barbara. A few campus staff went to his gatherings each spring. An admirer of JK who was in touch with a key staff member responsible for organizing his talks called her friend to arrange a luncheon meeting for Dhir with JK. Being educated in Varanasi, India, Dhir had heard JK's name, and the large organization called the Theosophical Society that he was associated with. This society operated a girls' college that was right across from Dhir's family home in an opulent neighborhood of Varanasi.

One day in 1909 when JK, at age eleven, was playing with his brother Nitya on Adyar Beach in Chennai, he was spotted by Mr. C. W. Leadbeater, an Australian clairvoyant who was a leader in the Theosophical Society hierarchy. He was struck by the luminous aura of the child. The esoteric masters of the Theosophical Society had instructed their disciples to be on the lookout for a saintly lad who was to appear in the world. One day, they found him. Dr. Annie Besant, an Englishwoman and the president of the Theosophical Society took the child under her protection. She gathered around JK a coterie of custodians to prepare him for a promising future. While JK was advancing intellectually, vast hierarchical organizations were being built to promote his teachings. Estates, lands, and endowments were gifted to him for his work. Devotees from all over the world flocked to be in his company.

Nonetheless, in 1929, JK dissolved the organization that was created for the coming world teacher, and all donations were returned. In 1933, Annie Besant died of natural causes. JK affectionately called her "mother," and with her passing, all his ties with the Theosophical Society came to an end. Free of any organization and all property and wealth, he set out to make humanity free of bondage, reliance, and dependency. Since then, JK traveled throughout the world, giving public talks to increasingly larger audiences. Worldwide, he was regarded as one of the great religious teachers, no less than Gautama Buddha himself! It was estimated that there were one million readers of JK's literature.

When he reached Chennai, India, in the fall of 1980, JK asked his local organizers of the Krishnamurti Foundation India (KFI) if Dhir could be invited to participate in a symposium with local scholars and Tibetan Buddhists.

It was Dhir's third notable trip back to India. One day, following the morning session and after lunch, Dhir walked with JK to his room and asked if he could organize a symposium in California. JK agreed to participate and asked him to make detailed plans with the Krishnamurti Foundation America.

In 1982, four dialogues were held with JK at his residence. During a three-day period, four groups—high school students, university students, high school teachers, and university professors—engaged JK in a dialogue on education and life. Among many of his postulates, JK brought the participants to focus on their viable nondualist approach to life. Since funds were secured from governmental sources, the entire videotaped symposia were transcribed, and a five-hundred-page report was prepared by Dhir. He wrote the introductory chapter, the prologues to the dialogues, and an extensive concluding chapter. A copy was sent to JK. He had to be impressed because, shortly thereafter, he called Dhir at his home to inquire about its publication. After extensive preparation, Dhir readied the manuscript for publication.

This book brought Dhir notoriety and a lot of inquiries. He was happy with how the project had been concluded. Some of the findings were incorporated into a new seminar course he had proposed to various curriculum committees on campus. A year later, Dhir was teaching that course as Children and Civic Values.

Also, several hypotheses had emerged during the preparation of the above manuscript. He incorporated those in a cross-cultural questionnaire protocol that was used by him in recorded conversations with children in two developed societies (the United States of America and the United Kingdom) and two developing societies (India and Taiwan). The resulting findings were included in two volumes; one was about educational environments in India, and the second analyzed the learned values of Chinese youth.

Throughout this period, Dhir felt uplifted by his scholarly endeavors. But whenever he would think of his immediate academic milieu, he would feel a bit let down. As time went by, the ideological battle intensified among the faculty, and it reached a harmful height by the early 1990s. The avowed conformists, both in faculty ranks and the administration, understandably succeeded in recruiting only their type of faculty—those who shared their mindset and would vote in the committees as a block to foster their dogma.

In an endeavor to bring diversity to their Anglo-dominated campus, as far as the administration was concerned, a new forthright vice president (who had a US Marines background), pushed the College of Social and Behavioral Sciences to accept an African American dean. After a great deal of arm-twisting, a dean was selected who did not fit the customary norm. It was not that the newcomer had any agenda— he was fair in his decisions—but the so-called White faculty members in general not only disliked him but also did everything they could to discourage him from succeeding as a dean. During his tenure, many positive curricular changes were made. Through proper channels, Dhir was appointed as the coordinator of Ethnic Studies program.

Although he was fully involved with the curricular growth of the Ethnic Studies program, he continued to teach all his courses, which he had taught from day one. These included International Relations and Comparative Third-World Development, as well as a social science capstone course entitled the Non-Western World that drew a large enrollment (in the hundreds). Also, his research led to his planning, compiling, and editing two issues for Crane Publishers on topics related to international conflict and terrorism.

Academically, all his allies were from outside his own department—Sociology, Psychology, Philosophy, and Theater Arts, to name a few. At the same time, when the department was not being affected curricular wise, there would emerge a shifting coalition. It was like the enemy's enemy was one's friend. For example, once, the outrageously partisan chair nominated Dhir for the position of coordinator of Ethnic Studies program simply because the most qualified candidate in the History Department was his staunch critic. Further, their new dean, who came from NYU, was an immigrant from South America and was being derided because of his race by a majority of the Anglo faculty from Social Sciences.

There were significant dissenters, including the women faculty members, who had their own priorities. Although they lobbied for hiring women in every department, they would object to hiring another woman in the same department. In general, they would bicker about the need to hire Brown and Black faculty. Certainly, that did not include men of the Middle East or the Indian subcontinent, as they falsely viewed these men as misogynist. Often, the older women put Dhir in that category, ignoring the fact that he was a die-hard supporter of women faculty.

The dean and Dhir became allies, primarily because they believed in fairness and summarily belonged to a non-White category. Such racial issues had not surfaced on this campus in the 1960s or even the 1970s. Now, they were rampant, like the smog.

During his preoccupation with the Ethnic Studies program, Dhir put together, with the help of his allies from several departments, an interdisciplinary Ethnic Studies minor program in African American Studies, Hispanic American Studies, Native American Studies, and Asian American Studies. The departments participating in this program were Art, Anthropology, Communications, English, History, Sociology, Social Work, Spanish, Music, Marketing, and Political Science. It was also during this time that Dhir published a major book on Asian Indian immigrants.

The same year, their African American dean departed for greener pastures. And a new dean arrived, an Anglo, who tended to pacify the White faculty members who were relishing the swap. The new dean went around getting acquainted with department heads and program coordinators. He came to Dhir's office as well. When asked how long he wished to continue chairing the Ethnic Studies program, discerning his intention to bring on board his own people, Dhir informed him, "Not any longer."

Following that, Dhir expressed to him his intention to retire.

The dean asked him his age and then said, "You are too young to retire."

But Dhir's mind was made up. Simultaneous to a languishing quality of academic life, he had undergone a personal life quandary in the mid-1980s that had dampened his spirit. It was, no doubt, a very stressful academic battlefield, in addition to his personal enigma. He wanted to return to a settled phase in the 1990s and create future plans. He would strive to seek peace and tranquility in the prime of his life. He was in his early sixties and had lived longer than his father and older siblings. Therefore, he felt he should take advantage of his good fortune while he was ahead.

Unlike some of his colleagues, who were going to work until the end, he wanted to bring his career to an end. Moreover, the academic environment was not going to tweak itself anymore. The entire raison d'être of higher education was taking a unique bent. The academe was modifying the liberal arts education and adopting the practical training courses like business, computer sciences, nursing, and paralegal studies that the two-year community colleges were consigned to teach. Because the market-oriented programs of study were becoming standard, students were singularly focused on enrolling in them, with the hope of securing a job, any job. The result was that in Social and Behavioral Sciences, where the focus was on analytical thinking, the patrons were the residuals who were not interested in any serious way in learning about problem solving. They just wanted a college degree, any degree. Undoubtedly, the tenet of liberal arts pedagogy was done for.

The original ethos of higher education that Dhir was exposed to prepared young men and women for citizenship, for enlightened leadership, for tackling the issues of society, and for enhancing their creativity. America had a tradition going back to Thomas Jefferson, who'd founded the University of Virginia, that a liberal arts education was the core of our democracy. If the nation were to lose an educated populace to some other persuasion, the people would be amenable to demagogy. The fear was that the professors would become propagandists. After all, many scholars like Dhir had come to North America for higher education and its fine centers of learning but felt betrayed now, abandoned, and indignant. They were now at the mercy of administrators who were focused on transforming American higher education into trade schools.

For the reasons elucidated above, but specifically due to the academe's new direction, Dhir began to nurture a serious mindset focused on postretirement lifestyle. Thinking of retiring was a mixed blessing. When his retirement arrived, would he be ready? Had he sufficiently prepared himself to make the most of it?

Some retirees-to-be may find themselves waiting to see what will happen once they enter retired life. Visions of relaxing while happily pursuing hobbies and passions filled Dhir's expectations. But adopting a wait-and-see attitude may not be the best course of action. He wanted to make a planned move. One's persona while working may not be replicated while in retirement. In fact, the skills that made one a likeable player on the job could be out of place in retirement. We need to recreate and redefine who we will be during our retirement years. Retirement can afford an opportunity to make changes, to try new things, and even to become the person we have always wanted to be.

In some societies, as in India, when people retire, they actually strive to give up their worldly desires. They practice renunciation. Their lifestyle changes drastically. They change their whole way of life. They even change their name and eliminate the titles they have earned. In other words, they pass from one phase of life to another.

When Dhir retired from teaching would he be able to create a new way of life for himself and change his mode of thinking about his life? It was tantamount to moving out of the sphere of achievement into the sphere of pastime, a stage of relaxation and appreciation of the wonders of living.

For married people, this phase of life can be particularly challenging. Ideally, they may have many years ahead to enjoy themselves in retirement. But he would also face new challenges along the way that might seem overwhelming. For example, a health issue for either of them would require them to depend on each other. What if one got sicker than the other? That was a dangerous phase.

There was also the possibility of becoming a widower or encountering financial problems. Although not always easy, it could help if he looked honestly at the facets of retirement that scared him the most. Rather than trying to ignore them, he must bring these potential issues to the attention of his spouse and discuss how he might prevent or cope with each challenge. As a united front, Dhir and his wife may be better equipped to face the issues the two of them would experience together.

If we retire at the typical age of mid-sixties, we are realistically moving into the later stages of our life. It is likely that we may be worn out after all the energy we have put into getting there. Neither would our health be the best it had been, nor would it likely improve as we continued living. With that in mind, it could make sense to live lavishly and even splurge, as opposed to saving it for the future. Whose future? At this age, there was no future; there was only the present.

Dhir and his spouse did take some more adventurous trips to Israel and the Gaza Strip, Spain, Portugal, and Morocco, along with numerous cruises. The same voyages would be too much of a strain at a later age.

One thing was sure; older people did become susceptible to

exploitation by unsuspecting relatives and unscrupulous neighbors and businesses, particularly in a state like Florida.

Changes in lifestyle were an absolute necessity as we get older. How could we entertain ourselves and yet be useful? Dhir made preparations to participate in hobbies and indulge in artistic urges before he retired, rather than waiting until retirement.

Another major undertaking for him was to plan for social development programs for the needy, such as eyesight recovery, hygiene projects, scholarships for indigent girls, and clothing for destitute pupils, especially in the remote villages of India.

In the 1990s as Dhir's mother entered her fragile old age, approaching a century, and becoming progressively frail, he began to visit her every year. It used to be a very grueling departure, as neither of them knew for sure if it would be their last meeting. Concurrent with his hometown visits, he and his wife intensified their social work, namely hygiene campaigns and eye clinics in northern India for the poorest of the poor.

Observing their earnest effort and their expenditure of huge sums of money, one day his mother asked him unpredictably, "What do you get out of this? What's in it for you?"

Before he could answer her, she smiled and said, "Your dad used to do this—I mean helping the needy."

Then Dhir understood not only that she approved of the work he and his spouse were doing in her hometown but also that she was testing whether he was doing it for the right reason.

In the beginning, social welfare projects have a tendency to boost one's ego and somewhat mitigate the higher goal they are intended for. At an early stage, such endeavors are partly self-seeking and partly egoless opus. None of us need be discouraged when we find that, in the early days, there is some motive of enlightened self-interest driving us on to a little social work. Without a motive in the beginning, social work would be difficult to initiate. Although there was a definite seed of religious motivation for Dhir and his spouse, there was a measure of personal motivation as well. Gradually, though, through numerous campaigns and often difficult problems they encountered with local volunteers, their personal motives were mollified, and an overwhelming desire emerged to uphold new opportunities for the deserving needy.

There were many factors in Dhir's early life that sowed the seeds for helping those who were less privileged than he was. First, there was his upbringing and the subtle messages he absorbed, along with watching what his significant role models were doing, namely what his father did in dealing with the downtrodden. Second, after his college days—when he entered the Hindutva's second stage of life in the traditional Indian scheme of things (namely, taking up a worthy occupation, marrying, and raising a family)—he felt privileged to enter a most satisfying occupation. He was privileged to work consecutively in two morally charged establishments; both were envisioned for helping the needy village folks.

These two village development experiences, along with his graduate research work, prepared him to look for opportunities to help the needy. In India, he gained social service experience in two institutions. The mission before Allahabad Institute near his hometown and the Cooperative Union in Delhi were similar. Both were engaged in rural development—a task that was totally neglected by the British while they ruled India. However, the justification and motivations at both institutions where he worked consecutively were markedly different. While the former was driven by a missionary zeal of healing the poor, the latter was guided by the Gandhian principles of forming one's character by serving the needy. According to Mahatma Gandhi, rural development ought to be normally undertaken to denote the actions and initiatives that would improve the standard of living in nonurban areas, especially remote tribal villages.

To reiterate, Dhir's enduring passion for social work made his transition to retirement much easier. He had much more going for him. Many people who work in the same career for decades invest their identity in it. That makes it difficult to retire, as, in their minds, losing their job makes them nothing. Dhir had no such qualms. He was happier not doing what his long years of postgraduate training had prepared him for. Now, he found a renewed passion for helping the needy.

Had Dhir's decision to retire been based on a thorough assessment of the balance of the positives and negatives of his working life? Yes, indeed. In the case of a mandated retirement, such a question is extraneous, but it isn't for those who contemplate early retirement as he did. Many of us may be inclined to focus more on the downside of our employment prior to opting for early retirement. For him, helping young people achieve their goals was outweighed by obvious negatives. Inducements to retire early were also a significant factor in making this decision. The California FERP (faculty early retirement program) allowed him to retire early while still working part-time for five years at a prorated salary.

Retirement, no doubt, is a challenging undertaking. Therefore, one of the biggest challenges for Dhir was what to do with all his spare time. The best avenue for him were to find leisure pursuits on campus where secure retirees were hanging out. As his first pastime, he enrolled in a class called printmaking, not knowing what it meant. But he liked it and got into the knack of making prints.

One day, he was reproducing copies of one of his projects when he heard someone call his name. It was the instructor who taught fine furniture making next door. He yelled, "Dhir, what are you doing here? You should be in my class."

So, he enrolled in the furniture making class as well.

He continued these two classes for five years until his FERP tenure ended and he moved out of state. As a farewell, his colleagues, the college dean, and the vice president took him to a local restaurant. There they properly thanked him for his thirty-five years of service to the university.

Some retirees would like to believe that their contribution to their career or vocation was significant or valued in ways that were not necessarily reflected by retirement parties, service plaques, emeritus desk paperweights, and disingenuous words from colleagues. Retirees often hear hackneyed speeches at trite farewell ceremonies and receive the traditional mass-produced gifts. These clichés can lead them to believe that this retirement ritual was a kind of perfunctory obeisance that leaves them feeling insignificant. This is not to say that those who arrange and administer retirement farewells are anything less than candid. Some might say that, if there is a problem, it lies with the retirees.

But if retirees experience a hindrance or a flaw in the institution's record keeping, they are justified in questioning the candor of the administrators involved. In Dhir's case, at first the administration failed to correctly account for his stated years of service. He had to prove the correct years of service by showing his appointment letter and a teaching schedule for the first term. Once the miscalculation was corrected via the president's intervention, he was invited the following year to the retirement party and was given a fake crystal for his thirty plus years of service to the university.

Most retired professors try to lead a stereotypical existence that makes no demand on their intellect and no use of a lifetime of experience. In order to change that, the beginning phase of Dhir's retirement had already begun when he enrolled in arts classes on campus. Many questions remained unanswered, though—the mythical retirement world, in which there is no loneliness, no worry, and no sickness and death, was a fairy tale. Dhir understood it to be just that. To anticipate the entire range of issues pertaining to retirement, the retreating entrants must explore categories of objective criteria—namely, activities, changeover, and crisis.

There are a number of vistas of human development that can shed light on the activities of one's past in shaping the meaningfulness of a retired life. Those who held a high executive or professional post in their occupation may have to move from the role of being a relevant employee to that of being an ordinary person. For all practical purposes, their roles and the social contact associated with them are also lost in retirement.

Aging is another source of role loss. Retirees may have reached a point where they can no longer continue with certain physical activities. They can compensate for the loss of some activities associated with their occupation by taking on tasks that are appropriate to their capacities. These may include joining service clubs, such as a Lions Club or Rotary International or attending places of worship.

In Dhir's case, he moved his residence to the opposite side of the country and lost contact with friends, relatives, neighbors, and colleagues. The impact of such a move could be more severe if the move involved a great distance. Moving to a place where the climate is warmer, health facilities are readily available, and places of interest are nearer is desirable. These benefits would tend to compensate for the loss of friendships and activities that have been built up over many decades.

Even though retirees can try to seek new friends and activities in a new environment, they are no substitute for the loss of long-term relationships and community involvement. Apart from the time it takes to develop a new circle of compatible friends, there is the problem of the energy required and the absence of roles that were once the medium by which social relationships developed.

Given the advancements in travel and communications, however, one need not suffer from the absence of long-distance friendships. Dhir continued to maintain his involvement with people and activities while living away.

Sudden changes in lifestyle are not easy to grapple. Therefore, one has to ascertain how much of what he or she did before can be continued. A continuity premise can also help people understand the smooth and gradual changes to their lifestyles. This idea is based on the fact that, although we live in the present, our existence is an extension of the past and an anticipation of the future. The changes that occur within our lives happen within the milieu of a continuous life span. Therefore, our life experiences are good predictors of our future, realizing that this does not mean we are necessarily trapped in our past. Change is inevitable, and we have to be ready for it and welcome it.

Continuities can either be internal or external. Whereas the former includes emotions, experiences, and dispositions, the latter involves relationships, clear actions, and efforts that are evident in our typical patterns of behavior. Most of us can track our changes from one stage to the next while being aware of the crunch. For being fully aware of our environment, internal continuity is necessary, in terms of self-image, self-worth, integrity, and the ability to cope with unexpected predicaments.

Also necessary is the external continuity of social strength. There is little doubt that retirees like Dhir would experience crises of continuity due to their retreat and changed ecology. Having been an emeritus professor for close to two decades, Dhir had acquired clear insights that could be used to navigate the flow of a retired life. Both the present and the future were endlessly reprioritized. This is a wonderfully dynamic stage of life. People must take pleasure in it while overcoming the hurdles as they come their way.

Carl Jung, a Swiss psychotherapist, labeled these various roles as personas that we assume when necessary. Clowns are great role players. The masks they wear represent a mood on a given day. Playing different roles is adaptive when it comes to making our way in society. It is a matter of behaving in an expected manner in various social situations—unless we wish to be an obscene nonconformist.

In retirement, the challenge of which part of our persona we wish to reveal remains, especially if we are striving to establish a new life in a new community. Do we have to be especially pleasant and outgoing? Or can we be our genuine selves, mean and cantankerous? Dhir fancied being somewhat dubious—good most of the time and ungenerous when it was necessary in dealing with obnoxious people!

Our sense of identity is more related to internal continuity than to our self-concept. For academics such as Dhir, self-concept is comprised of many thoughts or impressions related to academic vocation or taking pleasure in scholarship. We can have several selves but only one identity. Our notion of the self grows into generalizations that form our basic identity. For example, as a result of having a number of self-concepts that involve helping students or the needy poor, we may come to consider compassion as part of our identity. Sometimes, if we are accused of being heartless by exercising tough love, we might be tempted to defend ourselves with the claim that we are really kindhearted people. In this way, we can develop an identity that may be based on a discerning version of the past. This sort of behavior can occur when retirees such as Dhir begin to reflect nostalgically on their past. Changes to our identity occur throughout our lives, and we create them as situations warrant.

When Dhir entered his retirement stage, some of the experiences he encountered were unpleasant. At times, he was totally lost. At times, he was at the mercy of the bursar office and those who calculated his pension. Their slipups were a disruption in his internal continuity that led to an identity crisis. There were serious bureaucratic hurdles in Dhir's case as he was bringing his career to a conclusion.

One of the main experiences of Dhir's retirement was that he'd led a highly active and intense life before fully retiring and wanted to do so in retirement also. It seemed normal for him. He favored the idea of stability through continuity and understood that whatever he wanted to do in retirement should be established before he retired completely. As might be expected, involuntary retirees appear to have more difficulty adjusting to retirement than do voluntary retirees.

One might also add that those who can cope with changes in life probably transfer that capability to dealing with the ups and downs that are sure to occur during retirement. Because change is a fundamental aspect of human existence, those of us who have been able to ride the highs and lows of our preretirement life will be privy to the skills of coping with the move to retirement. There will be magic moments to enjoy, and then there will be mystifying flashes of past agonies. Our lives are punctuated with losses, as well as moments of fulfillment and happiness. Even our most treasured moments come and go. Nothing remains the same. It is the elemental ability to accept the rhythm of life that may be the best preparation for coping with the transition from full employment to partial retirement to no employment.

Undoubtedly, Dhir had led an excitingly unpredictable sojourn in America and had experienced good and bad. Yet, he had fulfilled his essential dreams, especially earning a doctorate degree, securing a chosen profession, and overcoming major hurdles in his family life. He was loved here and in India. He too loved his people here and there. He would not have traded his life for anyone. He'd made mistakes, no doubt. Who does not? We are simply human. Dhir did not want to be consumed with regrets. He wished few things had not happened. But it was all water under the bridge!

He had survived not only the usual challenges but also an unhinged student's bullet. One evening after finishing his classes, he'd headed home. As he made a right turn to drive up the hill, someone from a passing car shot at him point-blank. A 9mm bullet was lodged in the door frame four inches from his face. That incident was reported to the local police, and within six months, they found the culprit.

Unfortunately, there were other threats to his life, such as when his car flew off a mountain road at a curve and landed upright in bushes below in the ravine. He survived with chest injuries due to impacting the steering wheel. On another occasion, a rock was thrown at him that barely missed his forehead. There were many such incidents.

His trust in a higher power averted the dreadful end caused by these tragedies; indeed, the invisible hand of God had always protected or minimized the harm he might have otherwise faced. Often, he wondered how and why he'd escaped these annihilations if it were not for divine intervention. One has to agree that he was under the protection of a strong and resolute guardian angel.

On his part, it was his utmost desire to be honest with himself, to cultivate the skills of transparency and diligence, and to finish his own journey in a new country whose promises were spurious and largely jejune. But nothing was to be gained by holding on to bad experiences. Clinging to past wounds of India, where successful children were maligned by jealous kinfolk, or dealing with Canadian immigrants' "us-them" feeling or American indiscretion about foreigners would hinder his smooth transition into the blessings of his future.

Therefore, he decided to relinquish the pains of the past. But how do we do that? Can we forgive the person who hurts us? How? It is not a question of seeking a method but, rather, of feeling the impact of the hurt. Who is the source? Everyone who is insecure and fearful of others is a menace. By forgiving people who hurt us, we gain relief and peace of mind, irrespective of what happens to the perpetrator. By distancing ourselves from that evildoer and the harm he or she spews, will we gain freedom and relief? Yes! This we know.

To become conscious of this knowledge is a genuine achievement. It is the actual essence of breaking free from the bondage of our past, especially the hurts. Our past experiences may have prompted and formed us, making us the way we are, but we do not have to stay that way. By erasing the bygone, we can make room for the new and attain all good things of life.

Reflecting on his experiences, Dhir was reminded of a parable he had heard at a Baha'i gathering in New Delhi in 1956. Two monks were on a pilgrimage, and one day, they came to a river. At the edge of the river, a woman sat weeping because she was afraid to cross the river without help. She begged the two monks to help her. The younger monk turned his back because members of his sect were forbidden to touch a woman. But the older monk picked up the woman without a word and carried her across the river. Gently, he put her down on the dry shore and continued his journey. The younger monk came after him, scolding him and berating him for breaking his vows. He went on this way for a long time. Finally, the older monk turned to the younger one and said, "I only carried her across the river. You have been carrying her all day!"

Letting go of false beliefs, harmful ideas, deceptive expectations, injurious desires, and habits, and unhealthy relationships is necessary in order to move on with life's journey. Every day, every moment presents an opportunity to renew ourselves and shrug off the baggage of the past. It opens us to the possibility of the moment, of taking bold measures, and of creating an incredible future. Although we can understand this intellectually, being conscious of it and living it are two vastly different things. Dhir had to learn to live each day to the fullest and trust his creator completely. One of the blessings that came to his mind was the opportunity to reflect upon his life's good experiences. Life had been good to him. He doggedly meditated on God's abundant grace.

From birth to death, life is a continuous series of tensions or events moving around a nucleus of desires to live, create, enjoy, and think and, ultimately, to retire and rest. All of life's samskāras (totality of human conditions) and their rituals emanate from the center of life and are concurrent with its perimeter. Also, death is a fact of life. Life's journey is incomplete without its end.

A lifetime journey for a couple who have been together for six decades also comes to an end when one of them dies. In Dhir's case, it was his wife who passed away of heart failure. When a loved one dies, a part of us also dies. His life had been turned upside down. He became lonely and miserable and spent days and nights figuring out how to reconcile with the destiny of the death of a loved one. Waves of sorrow flooded his psyche until it crushed his resilience. So, he learned to surrender to the onslaughts of emotional pain by crying. Certainly, we can express our pain in tears. When we cry, we feel momentary relief. In the aftermath of a loss of this magnitude, there are no clear remedies and only opaque answers.

Ostensibly, life is a great mystery; its origin, growth, decay, and dissolution have always demanded our reflections and emotions. For Hindus of the Vedic era, samskāras were an attempt to fathom and to facilitate the flow of life's mystery. Through experience of the ages, the ancient Hindus edified that "being" was an art. It required cultivation, fine-tuning, and refinement. Born and left to itself, a human being was tantamount to an existence of a mass of elements—crude, brute, and removed from the incarnate beings. A human being's life stands in need of as much care, protection, and nurturing as a plant in a garden, crops in an open field, and a calf in a barn. The samskāras involve conscious efforts to meet human needs for dharmic (cosmic law) living. Wise men empowered with their enlightenment have inevitably tried to transform crude human proclivities found in nature into refined humanity and reconciled it with the sharp eventuality of death.

If Dhir's cremation were held tomorrow, who would come and what would they say? This question is the foundation of a genuinely great ending of a life's journey.

EPILOGUE

Every one of us has a story similar to this one. It could be inspiring, hilarious, romantic, surreal, or whatever. That is what this book comprises—a story within a story within a story. The narrative of this book was, in effect, chronological, personal, and analytical. Reference to actual people, events, or organizations was based on virtual facts rooted in reality. On purpose, it should offer a sense of validity. The events and circumstances are laid out judiciously. Most characters and numerous occurrences and conversations were a result of this author's existential and often critical reflections on the actual events. They ought not be construed as equivocal.

The story originated with the colonial beginnings of a young man born and raised in British India. Ruling nations as colonies were of many kinds. They were practiced under the guise of discovery and mercantilism, leading toward imperialism—in other words, establishing the superiority of the occupiers. Although colonialism, either Muslim or British, occurred in the past, it produced lasting positive as well as negative sways. The aftereffects linger in all cowed cultures, especially in South Asia, which was colonized for an awfully long period of time. These influences are syndromes—signs and symptoms—that are unique and indicative of mental mayhem. In particular, this is an unadulterated and unbleached depiction of a young man from a notoriously colonized India.

Keen observers of foreign rule have described the colonial mindset that can be grouped into four categories. First, there is the acceptance of foreign rulers, say the British, and their ways as superior. Second is an attempt to imitate a foreign culture in the hope of becoming like "them." Third is the attempt to absorb and act physically, culturally, and intellectually like their rulers and risk becoming strangers in their own homeland and misfits abroad. And fourth is risking a form of oppression that creates a perception of ethnic and cultural inferiority. In the case of India, even today, many intellectuals consider British colonialism as a form of benign oppression.

When this author was born, India had already been under British control for centuries, and the culture he was exposed to was not genuinely Indian. Symbols of foreign rule were everywhere—at home, in schools, in places of worship, and in the shops. Forged in a time of rapid industrial change when White European males assumed they ruled the world, others were simply mystified by their disingenuous claim. Yet, the long-term effects of that foreign grip on their consciousness could not be felt by anyone who had no experience of living under paranoid conditions.

After generations of such governance, beyond economic deprivations and political suppression, a people begin to lose confidence in themselves. Millions of Indians grew up with the belief that they were inferior and inept—born to be dictated by foreign rulers and, hence, not in control of their own destinies.

Consequently, the well-to-do citizens—the landholders, the doctors and lawyers, and certain upper levels of bureaucracy—sent their children to England or Canada. Ostensibly, they returned to careers in the bureaucracies of universities and colonial governments. Sometimes, in exasperation, they formed or joined an existing nationalist movement. In any case, it was self-evident that a road to success, personal or national, had to be a facsimile of the European ways. How long should such a master-slave bond have persisted?

A freedom from colonial rule, in any event, had to be in the form of a universal dialogue. The Euro-Christian and Euro-secular traditions that Judaic sources contested made it necessary for many scholars to examine and deal with the concept and practice of colonialism. In light of the Holocaust, new challenges emerged. The European philosophical tradition of negating modernity and defending the status quo, in which the dominant powers justified ruling the powerless and weak for the sake of world order, was thus contested. And it gave rise to a school of thought that also questioned the most original European thinkers of the twentieth century. In fact, their alleged affiliation with the Nazi regime revealed a serious bias in their thinking.

Emerged therefrom was a tradition of liberation theology that challenged the ideas of numerous conventional philosophers. Clearly, the link between ontology or a particular theory about the nature of "being" and power made the connection between "being" and the history of colonialism a heuristic enterprise. That gave rise to ample literature on the leitmotif.

The exploitation of the weak was deemed to be a long-term visible result of the denial of free will, and potentially, it had a deep-seated and enduring effect on their psyche. Hereafter arose the need to distinguish between colonialism and the colonial mindset; the latter endures and persists. Colonialism denotes economic and political relations in which the sovereignty of a nation (say India) or a people rests on the power exercised by another country (say Britain), which makes the latter an empire. Colonial mindset—namely, the unseen and seemingly benign subjugation—on the other hand, refers to long-standing patterns of power that take root because of colonialism. It defines the contours for the ruled people, as in the case of India, and shapes their culture, religion, social interactions, knowledge acquisition, work habits, and lifestyle.

In this way, the idea of colonial seizure of thinking was conceptualized during a discourse on its consequences over all walks of life and in different parts of society. It was felt that colonial relations of power would profoundly stain the dynamics of authority, knowledge acquisition, and economic activity. No doubt, it would have a lasting structural effect as well.

In other words, as subjugated "beings," we would be living a spurious life, a life denuded of the self. This was not just a construct; it was real. Thus, the idea of freedom backed by self-rule resonated so strongly with this author—who was until his college years abiding with the existence imposed by the rulers—that he became radically and intensely alien to his existence as a nonperson. Clearly, as he got older, he could not conform to any prescribed colonial norms.

Such outcomes, from the perspective of colonial otherness, revealed the true essence of colonialism of the mind. It provided an important clue to clarifying the specific ties between what the European philosophers referred to as "being" and the colonial project. There was still another thinker, Frantz Fanon, who interpreted ontology or human existence differently in a book entitled *Black Skin, White Masks*. The thesis therein not only provided the basis for an alternative depiction of the master-slave dialectic but also contributed to a more general rethinking of a way of subjugating other human beings. Might that not give rise to a search for decolonization measures for breaking the shackles of the oppressed and, hence, emancipating them?

Colonialism also introduced a notion that "whiteness" was an ideal to strive for. Teaching colonized people of color to idealize White skin perpetuated in them an inferiority complex and an inability to cope with everyday social situations, including personal relationships. Scholars have argued that the colonized mind sought to cast off its original skin and tried to occupy the skin of the colonizer. Scholars have used psychoanalytical theories to explain the feelings of inadequacy and dependency that people of color experienced in a White world. There emerged a divided self-perception of the non-White subjects who lost their native cultural uniqueness by getting into the art, music, and literature of the occupiers. This tendency, as contended by Fanon, had permeated the entire colonial society, impacting even the untutored and, certainly, the upwardly mobile educated class.

Mind-altering foreign rule, in its final phase, became the self-correcting behavior, especially among the young aspiring Indians who were susceptible to the trappings of the White culture. At the same time, it affected the traditional elite, who could not help but accept the authority of a foreign ruler because of the immediate benefits in the form of status, spurious titles, and tax rebates. Such mechanisms were designed to create separate classes of people, especially in the rural areas. Naturally, they lost all those privileges in light of the postcolonial reformations.

Eventually, the true losers of India's freedom from the British were the traditional elite, also called zamindars. Whenever this author visited his village home, he noticed a marked change in his uncle, who looked after their landed property. His uncle never recovered from land reform in independent India—being free of a foreign rule did not suit him. He took India's rejection of a foreign ruler as a personal loss of property and prestige. It is sad that he was not alone in this category of imbecile natives.

Strangely, the older generation, in their own way, tried to groom the younger generation to become like the White colonizers. However, their offspring's desire was to be selective of certain aspects of Western culture. They were not only risk-takers but also probers of what was not reasoned through.

In any event, the colonized mind in India was obsessed with the foreign frame of mind, where everything external to one's history and culture was deemed desirable. Before his departure for Canada, this memoirist's colleagues in Delhi issued a diktat: "Thou shall indulge in the White skin but not marry the person and bring her home."

In fact, their veiled normalized protests were lucidly described. Why should they accept someone's claim of superiority? Why is it that part of humanity considers others to be less than human? Are these claims based on a sense of divine superiority or on a fear that others might be better or could become better than them or even far excel over them? Could it be that the White race is incapable of hard work? It is known that even the devil can cite the scriptures to claim his dominance.

Based on mercenary, egoistic, and selfish reasons, the White race considered the Blacks as inferior, and hence, slavery came into vogue. The so-called inferior races, targeted primarily because of the color of their skin, were judged as subordinate to the superior White race. Even after the abolition of slavery and civil rights legislation passed by the Congress of the United States, White supremacy has persisted. It depends on who monitors and controls the wealth and power. The supremacists control the riches, and the downtrodden remain as they were before the hubbub.

Amazingly, the fact remains that young people from former colonial countries were virtually oblivious to the subtleties of North American life, culture, and history. They had made a leap, and nothing was going to stop them from a foreign sojourn. No amount of suffering caused by the barbarities of colonialism could excel marginalization and the culture of bigotry, sexism, racism, and intolerance. Shunning those, they ventured and arrived in the Western countries for education.

These pro-foreign youth, also known as the xenophiles, were cheering themselves and were engaged in narcissistic self-admiration. Obviously, their denial, albeit lack of knowledge, of the social imperatives of a new society they were about to enter would eventually impact their identity, as well as their psyche. Yet, no one was going to deprive them of their resolve to study and live abroad. When people overlook the reality of an unfamiliar society and its egotistic norms and values, not only are their expectations affected but also their overall growth is stunted. In the long run, they will be satisfied with neither themselves nor their surroundings.

Employing this line of thinking, Fanon deploys the existential expressions of mind's acquiescence in relation to imposing a foreign lifestyle in its racial and gendered dimensions. That, rightly, focuses our attention on the trauma of encountering the imperial power and its weapon of racism. Colonial subservience blatantly raises the challenge of connecting the natural and historical dimensions where life exhibits most evidently its imperial side and its gravitas. As was argued earlier, since altered thought patterns survive even the end of colonialism, colonial mindset blossoms in scholarly works, in cultural milieu, in common sense, in people's self-image, and in how men treat women. In a way, as modern subjects, we breathe colonial values, norms, and lifestyle all the time, every day. It is not simply the aftermath or the residue of any given form of dominance; it becomes an internally fixed feature of our mind, twisting our reasoning and thought patterns.

This relationship between the conquerors and the conquered, grounded in the idea of a domineering race, places a given people in a natural situation of inferiority to others. If so, then they conjure to join them in their own game at the intellectual level. Maverick younger generations of the ruled found a so-called easy way to be like them—or to be better in their own socioeconomic environment. For them, higher education in Europe, Canada, or America was one such modus operandi.

Thus, to be virtually free of exclusion, one could be in the company of their superiors. Yet the race issue made them a cosmetically inferior being—a truly catch-22 dilemma! We are part of a system of domination structured around the idea of a superior race. This race model of power is at the heart of the modern experience. Modernity, usually considered as an outcome of European Renaissance and the European Enlightenment, has a darker side, its upshot. Modernity as a discourse and as a practice would not be possible without colonialism's lasting impact. Seemingly, this syndrome continues to be an inevitable sequel of modern homily.

A characteristic feature of this type of social dialogue is that the relationship among the subjects is not horizontal but, rather, vertical, and non-equal in character. That is, some identities depict superiority over others. And such superiority is premised on the degree of humanity attributed to the identities in question. The lighter one's skin is, the closer to full humanity one is and vice versa. The idea has persisted that non-Europeans have a biological structure that was not only different from that of Europeans but also inferior in essence. This differentiation was indelibly etched on intersubjective relations and social practices of European society.

In large measure, scientific racism and the very idea of ethnicity were the most explicit expressions of a widespread and general insolence regarding the humanity of colonized and caged subjects in the world of the sixteenth century. Therefore, it is appropriate to suggest that what was conceived in that century was something far craftier and more permeating than what at first appeared in the concept of a superior race. It was an assertion meant to be a permanent misgiving, in that a European might ask a colonized person, "Are you completely human?" Is it not ironic that the descendants of Neanderthal—crude, dumb, hideous, hostile, and ugly morons—have playacted to acquire superiority through the accident of the climate of their birth in a temperate zone!

It turned out that, "You have rights," became, "Why do you think you have rights?" Likewise, to deny humanity, an oppressor might ask, "Are you really a poised person?" Such a scathing suspicion is like a maggot at the very core of modernity. This causative rationality operates within the logic that disdainful cynicism helped to establish prodigious rules over the perceived feeble. That is why the idea of progress as modernity was advanced for a few and why the rights of human beings did not apply equally to all. Incredulous as it is, it affords the basis for the option that explains why security for some can plausibly be achieved at the expense of the lives of others. After all, wars are fought on the territories of the fragile and vulnerable.

The imperial attitude of the superpowers fostered a fundamentally genocidal proclivity in respect to racialized and marginalized people. Through it, the subjugated people of the third world were marked as weedy and dispensable. Need for battle, conquest, and genocide highlighted another fundamental aspect of colonial conquest; that is, it created suspicions with regard to the foreign peoples having a soul. Lacking a credulous soul, might they not be better off excising their old ways for a new—say, the European way? That is what the American Indians had to do to survive.

Even today, middle-class families in non-Western societies send their children to convent schools, where the instruction is in the English medium, and curriculum is syncretic and biased toward the

Western ways. Here, the goal of the institution is to raise children in so-called modern ways that will be flexible and adaptable to varying environments. In fact, the author came across schools in the state of Kerala, India, that boasted of their specialized curriculum that prepared students to take up jobs abroad. However, their reach was confined to Dubai, Qatar, and Saudi Arabia, where there was a desperate shortage of middle-level professionals.

After India achieved her independence from the British, there emerged a mindset that focused on bringing home the European and North American technical education and scientific know-how. On every conscientious Indian mind was the urgency of bringing home technical know-how and making the country prosper. This is what the leaders had in mind, particularly Prime Minister Jawaharlal Nehru, in setting up in every state of the new country at least one Indian Institute of Technology (IIT). Lamentably, quite a number of those India-trained techies escaped to find gainful employment in places like the Silicon Valley of California, United States of America.

But for the early sojourners, the forerunners like this author, a question remained: Where to go for foreign education? The choices were limited to the United Kingdom, Canada, or the United States. Given that India had just achieved independence from Britain, it was not proper to go there. And the United States was not only an inhospitable pick, but also one had to endure many hurdles—among them difficulties in receiving student visas and the need to make a huge deposit as collateral. So, the choice was Canada, also a dominion of the British Empire but free of the facets of colonial regime as in India. There was probably no part of the world where the conditions for affecting profound changes in the social order and development of right ideas were more favorable than in Canada.

Way back in the 1900s, Indians, along with other Asians, were targeted by American bigots as a threat to their country. The San Francisco-based Japanese Korean Exclusion League changed its name to Asiatic Exclusion League to include immigrants from China and India.

Our people were deemed by these bigots as cheap labor, dangerous, and unassimilable. Ironically, they believed that the independence India was demanding from the British would jeopardize US national security.

As a result of the exclusion and practice of discrimination, a widespread violence occurred against the innocent foreigners from Asia. Especially, people from India were not only harassed and prohibited from owning or leasing land; they were also chased out of many towns and cities on the West Coast. Hostilities intensified in the wake of the 1911 decisions of the US Immigration Commission and the Immigration Act of 1917. The latter created the Asiatic Barred Zone, which officially excluded half a million people of Asia. It was an accepted fact in Asia that Americans were unbearably devoted to their own opinions and prejudices, mainly when it came to people of color. They confronted all non-Whites with hatred and intolerance.

The heart of the argument was White supremacy, which seemed like a narcissistic disorder—lacking empathy and showing paranoia about losing privileges and a spuriously reputed place in their world. It was not until the Immigration and Naturalization Act of 1965 that the doors were opened for Asians. Also known as the Hart-Celler Act, it abolished an earlier quota system based on national origin and established a new policy focused on reuniting immigrant families and attracting skilled labor into the country, especially the IIT graduates mentioned earlier.

In British India, it was Lord Macaulay's plan to create a race that was "English in taste, but Indian in color." He created a sense of inferiority among South Asians by exploiting their insecurities emanating from their caste and skin color. Now in the postcolonial era, by leaving their native land, young people, including this author, were made to believe they were rising above their sense of inferiority. Their parents, peers, and guardians in India, raised under the shadow of colonialism but not yet sovereign in mind, promoted the European dream, at least for the next generation. They saw Western education for their offspring as an opportunity to transcend a colonial mindset and gain prosperity, as well as prestige, for the family. There appeared a great promise indeed. But did they not obtain a confused and misplaced youth who would belong to neither cultural milieu?

No doubt Macaulay's pathetic plan created an enduring postcolonial world. At the same time, there were righteous thinkers who reasoned differently. For example, Sir Edmund Burke, a noted philosopher, and a distinguished member of the parliament was a staunch opponent of English rapacity in India, though he supported the British Empire.

Regrettably, the culpability of the Indian youth played into the hands of the colonizers. Rather than achieving obtainable goals above and apart from the colonial mindset, they strove to be just like them. Those anglophiles, with outrageously non-native tendencies, having acquired daring goals, also pushed themselves toward seeking a foreign lifestyle. The primary passion and purpose for their going abroad was to be educated in a Western society that professed belief in freedom for the deserving and was not marred and blighted by the rules and regulations of a foreign ruler.

Added to that was a continuous family encouragement and peer expectations that compelled them to leave their homeland. Inferred was an implicit sense of personal freedom, of great promise, and of serendipitous opportunity. Unreservedly, this move, they hoped, could provide a way to penetrate and surmount the world of their oppressors. They would likely mingle with them, attend classes with their children, and might become part of them even at the periphery. For a local merchant in town, it was to situate himself in a marketplace where he could practice a monopolistic trade. This would also upgrade his lifestyle. He whispered that he moved here to be where the lavish White people lived.

In the 1960s, a Berkeley professor declared that she had migrated to the West with a view to assuming the role of a neo-conqueror. That is, she moved to America to bring about a social change, to open the doors, and to win over people—not just to acquire a White husband. In general, people were fearful of immigrants who looked different than themselves. She was right, in that many, including this author, were eventually successful in winning over many of the natives. And they, in turn, won over the new Asian Indians as well. Some of them married their sons and daughters and raised upright families who were proud of their dual heritage.

The population of Asian Indians in the United States is very small, given the fact that they represent the crème de la crème. This community is also fairly successful, with the median household income almost twice that of typical households. Immigrants from India are more likely a product of higher education; they are willing and able to participate in the labor force and twice as likely to be employed in academia, management, business, science, high tech, and the arts.

In particular, Indian Americans in the United States are challenging the establishment; they are cracking the traditional power bastions that, for immigrants, can often be virtually impenetrable. What is particularly notable, however, is the heightened degree of political engagement and activism that immigrants from India display. This diaspora, over recent decades, has become increasingly involved in US politics; in addition, a number of political action groups have sprung up, aiming to promote the voices of their members. At last, they are learning to challenge the system that has been marginalizing them.

This mindset is, no doubt, antithetical to what Macaulay's plan was for the colonized youth of a downtrodden nation. These convivial gestures would have infuriated him. These vagaries as they have evolved, one can safely assume, have provided to some Indian immigrants an opportunity that the colonial rulers could not afford. At last, it must have made Macaulay and his brand turn in their graves!

Surely, America has been a promised land for European immigrants. For them, it was a wealthy country that embraced them and offered them solace and a prosperous life span. However, many other immigrants, especially those from third world countries, do not feel appreciated here. That is why they continue to make frequent trips to their places of birth while living here. It's why they live in their own ghettos here. It's why their social circles are confined to those of their own kind.

For them, America is not the melting pot where identity and culture were preserved but, rather, a searing serving dish where aspirations and dreams were boiled away. Not only were their dreams not entirely fulfilled in coming to America, but ironically, their identity and culture tended to vanish in the country of the potentials.

This country is predominantly for White people, most specifically for preordained White Anglo-Saxon men. History, which has favored the United States for two centuries, could pass America by if the disparities continue. In view of the rapid progress in Asia and elsewhere, America cannot remain the world's most dynamic economy or even a middle-class society. The American dream could turn into an American nightmare of economic stagnation, demise of democracy, and breeding ground for xenophobic leaders that could cause havoc by endorsing a racially charged pecking order.

Why it is that people of color are viewed as not belonging to America? Even if they are born here or have lived as either an immigrant or a citizen for decades, they are often asked, "Where are you from? Have you been home recently?"

The answer, according to one testimony, may lie in the fact that this is a country meant for the "right kind." In any normal conversation, racism, and sexism, sooner or later, does pop up. It is one of the few Western countries where even women face hurdles building up to the highest post. Is it in the nation's DNA? Sneering of foreign-looking people aside, two notably damaging and enduring assaults have shaken the spirit of immigrants of color. They could never feel safe here.

Of late, two notable tragedies that shook the lives of people of color, especially those of brown color, were: (1) the Iranian hostage crisis, and (2) the suicide attacks by Islamic extremists on the Pentagon and the Twin Towers of New York City.

When Iran's deposed Shah was allowed to come to America for cancer treatment in October 1979, the Ayatollah followers attacked the American embassy in Tehran, and its employees were held captive for 444 days. However, the hostage-taking was about something more than the autocratic Shah's medical care in the United States. It was a dramatic way for the student revolutionaries to declare a break with Iran's past and end the American interference in their national affairs. It was also a way to raise the domestic and international profile of the revolution's leader, the Ayatollah Khomeini. At last, the students set their hostages free just hours after President Ronald Reagan delivered his inaugural address.

During the hostage era, on two occasions, this author was yelled at by White youth. "You don't belong here. Go home. Go to your country."

He asked them, "Whose home? I live here. I was here when you were born."

That slight was benign compared to what followed.

On September 11, 2001, highly trained militants associated with an extremist Islamic faction hijacked four airplanes and carried out attacks against targets in the United States. The 9/11 assaults comprised of a series of airline hijackings that were flown into high-rise buildings by a bunch of Brown-faced terrorists associated with the Islamic extremist group, Al-Qaeda. It was the deadliest terrorist attack on US soil; nearly 3,000 people of roughly 145 nationalities were killed. The impact of this calamity went far beyond geopolitics; it shook the norms of society and humanity in general. Immediate responses to 9/11 included greater focus on home life and time spent with family; higher church attendance; and increased expressions of patriotism, such as the flying of American flags and boycotting French fries.

For unsuspecting Americans of color, it was a different story—a scary and daunting existence. Enhanced physical and mental attacks were carried out against them. Many turbaned Sikhs from India were gunned down. Even in shopping malls, angry Americans would shout abusive language into the faces of those who did not look like them. On streets and highways, they would ram into their cars from behind.

Students from the Middle East stopped attending classes because several of them were bludgeoned to death in the parking lots of their apartment. Even the police were picking on them. For at least a month, non-White people were afraid to leave their homes. Some of their sympathetic neighbors brought groceries for them. Students were not penalized for not attending classes in the universities and were mailed take-home examinations.

During those days, this author had his home on both coasts and, hence, was traveling between Los Angeles and Miami every three months. Being White, his wife did not, but he had to go through extra security checkups each time. Once, he was shocked to experience a totally bizarre quirk; the TSA agent at MIA yanked his wallet from the back pocket of his trousers and began to go through his driver license, insurance card, and credit cards. He gave the agent a scornful look and said to himself, *Whither has gone the American Bill of Rights? What's happened to "search and seizure" prohibition?*

There is nothing ingenuous about this society after all. How can people's civil rights be respected in this paranoid country? Has bin Laden changed this society for the worse? Apparently, he did!

These two atrocious acts of familiar domestic terrorism have tended to normalize violence against foreign-looking Americans. Of course, White men have been involved in assassinations of presidents and other famous leaders and even domestic bombings of federal buildings. But these incidents were all treated as aberrations. Was the January 6, 2021, insurrection, and forceful entry into the US Capitol, where domestic rioters were about to hang the elected leaders, a benign rally?

Once hate-motivated killings of immigrants of color became a common occurrence in the early 1990s, the Federal Bureau of Investigation began collecting data officially. The FBI defined hate crimes as those motivated by bias and based on a person's race, religion, or sexual orientations. It wasn't just the populations of color who were subjected to hate; Jews and Jewish institutions were also targeted. During the last four years, Mexican Americans were particularly besieged because of their influx at the southern border. One reporter claimed that the US Department of Health and Human Services had lost track of nearly fifteen hundred immigrant children. They were allegedly separated from their parents at the border. A baffling photo appeared depicting two adrift immigrant children behind a chain-link fence.

One day, Dhir's new neighbor in Florida asked him about his nationality and immediately avowed, "You're from India, aren't you?"

He replied, "Yes, and I am proud of it." Then he asked her, "You're from Poland, aren't you?"

She responded, "Yes. We are the wanderers. To escape the Nazis, we ran to Romania, became Catholics, and later migrated to the United States in 1965."

He did a mental calculation and concluded that he had been here longer than she had been. Yet in her mind, he was a foreigner, and she was a typical American hoisting a red, white, and blue flag in her front yard. He also belonged here, perhaps more than she did because of his notable contributions to American society.

When he was sworn in as a naturalized citizen in 1969, he pledged his loyalty to the Constitution of this country. Many Americans, especially of European descent, tend to possess multiple passports. Obviously, they have a divided allegiance, as they had to swear to be loyal to other countries that granted them citizenship. Not only does US law not mention dual nationality, but it does also not require a person to choose one nationality over another. But this author holds only American citizenship and is loyal to this country only.

Working hard in the competitive system of American higher education, he earned a master's degree and a PhD. He has raised a family here who also loves and respects this country's institutions. For three and a half decades, he has taught at two different universities, where a total of about fifteen thousand students have listened to his lectures and acquired mental skills from him. Over three and a half decades, he mentored thousands of students of different races, colors, religions, and political persuasions. These students have graduated to go on to become lawyers, doctors, professors, entrepreneurs, public servants, administrators, and public-school teachers.

He and his family have paid their taxes at the local, state, and national levels. They have actively participated in civic and community life for more than half a century. Even then, they have often been dismissed as irrelevant, marginalized, and rendered less important than a White-faced American.

In spite of these foibles, they belong here. And they have earned their right to live here by dint of their hard work, endurance, socialization, and love of the country.

Although America's record of social progress is sporadic, it still holds a promise for a dynamic society, where immigrants in general do bring fresh ideas. So far, they have sacrificed comfort and adhered to hard work. Commendably, aided by the workforce from abroad, America rescued capitalism under Franklin Roosevelt and Harry Truman. It restored humanity to Black Americans under JFK and Lyndon Johnson through civil rights legislation. We were told by them that immigrants in America were becoming a part of the most promising and avant-garde nation on earth.

Today, we know what was odious about a promised-land rendering of American history. It left out the absolute horrors of slavery, genocide, dislocation, and annihilation of native Indians and Black Americans. Of course, there were others who suffered, such as the Asians, who bore the collateral damage. Lamentably, this nation often becomes victim of racial hysteria—as when it interned innocent Americans of Japanese ancestry. The sad truth is that such travesties are often repeated because, in response to global affairs, this nation's culture of bigotry and racism manifests its ugly past. Be that as it may, predictably the United States of America, in spite of its evil past and the present chaos, is, for the most part, an experiment in pluralistic republicanism.

Notwithstanding its volatile history, America continues to be touted as a beacon of freedom and democracy that captivates people from the non-Western areas of the world. No doubt, they piggybacked here on the coattails of the Anglo-Saxon immigrants. While the latter moved here en masse to make a home, non-White immigrants mostly entered the halls of higher learning to educate themselves. Their goal was to go back home, largely because of the cultural pull and family commitments. It wasn't that they wouldn't have wished to stay longer and earn valuable experience in the workplace, but it was tricky to find dignified pockets of workplaces that would openly welcome non-European foreign nationals. They hesitated to prolong their stay here because of unease on both sides. Mostly, it was a lack of assimilation due to cultural variances and bigotry.

Unfortunately, ignorance about people from the non-Western world has been systemic. In a society where there is just one litmus test for the quality of humanity, we all become racially sensitive and gauge even our own kind with the same faulty measure. Then what is the difference between us and our oppressors?

There seems to be an abiding theme as to how outsiders are treated in a society such as this one. It is a unique conditioning or socialization involving a Pavlovian mindset. Foreign students, therefore, should be encouraged to familiarize themselves with a book like one of Steinbeck's. Almost a century ago, John Steinbeck, in his *Grapes of Wrath*, described a calamitous combination of drought and the chronic economic depression that compelled its victims, the sharecroppers of Oklahoma's dust bowl, to start a new life in the promised land of California. Steinbeck narrates the cruelty and prejudice the struggling migrants faced throughout their long journey. At their destination, those promises were broken. The victims were left stumped.

Steinbeck's depiction showed once again how the early arrivals of each generation of immigrants were treated. The settled immigrants of yesterday had now not only forgotten their own struggles but had lost touch with their humanity and the moral lessons of caring and sharing. Every wave, every generation of immigrants had to go through the cruelty of struggles and neglect that illuminated the spineless character of American society.

The moral dilemma we face today is also captured in another book, *American Dirt* by Jeanine Cummins. *The Grapes of Wrath* and *American Dirt* reveal the fate of new immigrants; they are treated as less than human and a menace to US economy and society. How can one forget that, not too long ago, the ancestors of now prosperous Americans came from other lands, mostly Europe? Likewise, they were abused and dehumanized. They were deemed uncivil. When did they, the assimilated immigrants, start believing they were better than the new arrivals? Why did they not understand that the newcomers came here because they had the same aspirations and values as the earlier arrivals? Otherwise, they would have gone somewhere else. Ostensibly, Steinbeck and Cummins have both diagnosed the prevailing antipathy perpetrated by deranged politicians who remain shortsighted and xenophobic.

Graduate students from abroad should also be advised to stay away from aiming to earn a degree in culturally dubious fields. Graduates of certain major fields in agricultural sciences are not going to be gainfully employed here. Sensibly, this also applies to defense and intelligence areas. An exception to picking an area of expertise in these subjects may be for those who have liens on their jobs at home and will return upon earning their diplomas. There are always serendipitous outcomes when personal lifestyles are concerned, including who might be one's life partner.

The xenophobic thinking of the average American creates an atmosphere of concern that discourages third world immigrants from making long-term plans. However, those who come just for education often strive for a brief work experience. That amounts to an additional aptitude for seeking a suitable job when they return home. Inequity, as was applied to foreign students, was not always odious and outright racist. Their qualifications and competence were adequate for appropriate jobs here and in their homeland. But they faced hurdles that discouraged them from settling down here. They were told that, by seeking a job, they would likely muddle the competition. America's just compass has always been fragile, and the great promise was not universally applied.

Luckily there were caring and compassionate Americans, though discrete, who had traveled abroad and were open-minded. These thoughtful Americans often fought off the xenophobes and the racists in return for a complaint-free allegiance to the country's noble ideals. But the rural, poorly educated, and unenlightened masses were heartless, self-centered, and spiteful. Ostensibly, the sane and angelic Americans came to rescue the underdogs. But one had to be in the right place at the right time. In the shadow of these seraphim lay the salvation for the third world students. Under their protection, they completed their education and even participated in the American dream. In the end, through persistence and hard work, many of the aspiring and forbearing foreign students have created a niche for themselves. That turned out to be more conducive to their reachable ambitions, as in this author's case, than it would have been in the traditional and regressive societies they would have returned to after a superfluous foreign education.

After completing their stay abroad and returning to their homeland, foreign students face numerous challenges; foremost is the phenomena known as reverse culture shock, which is similar to what this chronicler experienced in a foreign country when he arrived there. Isn't it ironic that he was feeling out of place in his own homeland, where everything around him should have been familiar? That was the time when he lamented his decision to study abroad; moving back home was getting quite tricky, requiring reintegrating into local ways, strange behaviors, a slow pace, and a nonchalant lifestyle.

Realistically, though, returning foreign students should look at it as an opportunity to rediscover their homeland with a new perspective. After an adventure abroad, one's daily life might not feel stagnant once he or she is settled. Surely, with new technology, the globe has shrunk, and it is easier now to stay in touch with friends and relatives abroad. Eventually, it will dawn on these returning students that they are not just a citizen of one country; they now belong to the world.